EXPLORER

Editorial

Authors	Carole Harris
	Tony Schroder
Editor	Pamela Grist
	Pamela@Explorer-Publishing.com
Editor (1st Edition)	Katie Hallett-Jones
	Katie@Explorer-Publishing.com

Sales & Advertising

Advertising Manager	Hema Kumar
	Hema@Explorer-Publishing.com
Advertising Executive	Wendy Menzies
	Wendy@Explorer-Publishing.com
Corporate Sales	Nadine Laurent
	Nadine@Explorer-Publishing.com

Production & Design

Layout	Jayde Fernandes
	Jayde@Explorer-Publishing.com
IT & Layout	Derrick Pereira
	Derrick@Explorer-Publishing.com
Designer	Pete Maloney
	Pete@Explorer-Publishing.com

Distribution

Distribution Manager	Ivan Rodrigues
	Ivan@Explorer-Publishing.com
Distribution Executive	Abdul Gafoor
	Gafoor@Explorer-Publishing.com
Distribution Executive	Mannie Lugtu
	Mannie@Explorer-Publishing.com

Administration

Publisher	Alistair MacKenzie
	Alistair@Explorer-Publishing.com
Administrative Manager	Yolanda Rodrigues
	Yolanda@Explorer-Publishing.com

Photographer	Carole Harris
Printer	Emirates Printing Press
Website	Internet Solutions

Explorer Publishing & Distribution

Dubai Media City   Phone 391 8060 Fax 391 8062
PO Box 34275, Dubai   info@explorer-publishing.com
United Arab Emirates   www.explorer-publishing.com

ISBN 976-8182-36-9
First Published 2001
Second (Revised) Edition 2002
Copyright © 2002 Explorer Group Ltd

Int~~roduction~~

Cong...
Unde...
local ...
design...
Explore...
ly dived ~~...~~ ... is also *a means of passing on invaluable local dive knowledge that would otherwise take years to discover.*

All photography in the guide has been taken locally, with the dive shots by Carole Harris, one of the authors. The drawings and maps are by Tony Schroder, the co-author.

*The **Underwater Explorer** is not intended as a dive training manual. This is a guide to enable divers of all abilities to make the most of the diving available around the UAE. Details of dive companies are included at the back of the book.*

*We hope you enjoy the **Underwater Explorer** and that it encourages you to sample the many stunning dive experiences awaiting you in the waters of the United Arab Emirates. If you have any comments about the book, we would be extremely grateful to hear from you; reader feedback has always been an integral part of the process of improving and evolving any Explorer guide.*

Teach others to be responsible divers and to respect the delicate world surrounding them. It's a long journey back to shore and a recompression chamber! Happy Diving!

Carole, Tony and the Explorer Team

A big thank you to our sponsor

محمـــــد بـن مســـعـــود واولاده
MOHAMMED BIN MASAOOD & SONS

Distributors of

The Authors

Carole Harris

Hailing from Portsmouth, UK, Carole always dreamt of diving underwater but the cold UK waters were neither inviting nor appealing.

Carole learnt to dive in 1986 with the BSAC 406 Club, based in Sharjah. She obtained her BSAC Advanced Instructor qualification, then completed her PADI training up to Dive Master. From diving sprung yet another passion, that of underwater photography. She has an impressive selection of equipment, including several Nikonos V cameras and a Nikon F801. As well as supplying the underwater photography for the Underwater Explorer, she has had numerous pictures published in a variety of books, magazines, calendars and newspapers.

Carole has been resident in the UAE for the last 17 years. Having completed more than 2,000 dives, the majority of these in UAE waters, Carole can be found under the water more often than not!

Tony Schroder

Born in Argentina, Tony grew up mainly in England. It was probably the five years he spent with his family stationed in the former colony of Malaya that sparked his great interest in nature. His love of the sea has also been a life-long affair and snorkelling gear an absolute essential on every trip.

His first experience of diving was with the Jebel Ali BSAC 916 Club in 1988. He is now a BSAC First Class Diver and Advanced Instructor with the BSAC 1339 club. As long ago as 1990, Tony started collecting information on wreck sites. The purchase of a GPS in 1991 opened up even more possibilities for locating wrecks and dive sites.

Tony is an explorer at heart and when he is not investigating submerged wrecks, he enjoys 4 wheel driving and off-road trips. He has lived in Dubai for 22 years with his wife Christine. He would love all divers to share in the pleasure this pursuit has given him.

Table of Contents

Explorer's Latest Products

Dubai Explorer

Now in its seventh edition, the Dubai Explorer is firmly established as the leading annual lifestyle guidebook to Dubai.

Comprehensive, fun and easy to use, this book covers everything worth knowing about Dubai and where to do it. Meticulously updated by a resident team of writers, photographers and lovers of life, the result is the most in-depth, practical and accurate coverage of Dubai. This is the insiders' guide to what's hot and what's not in Dubai and the Emirates! Ideal for residents, short-term visitors, business people and tourists, the **Dubai Explorer** is an essential resource for anyone exploring this vibrant and surprising city.

Off-Road Explorer (UAE)

20 adventurous off-road routes...

The **Off-Road Explorer** is the only off-road publication with clear and simple maps that are designed for the non-map reader, but which have the accuracy and detail of cartographic maps. Using satellite imagery, every stage of the route is superimposed with the correct track to follow. For each route, points of interest are highlighted, along with distances and advice on driving the more difficult parts. Remarkable photography peppers this guide, and additional information on topics such as wildlife, safety tips, and archaeology complement the off-road routes.

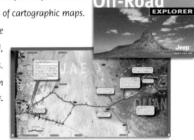

Family Explorer (Dubai & Abu Dhabi)

This is the only family handbook to Dubai and Abu Dhabi.

With increasing numbers of families visiting or relocating to the region, the new **Family Explorer** (previously the **Kids Explorer**) is the perfect resource for those wanting to make the most of their stay, whether long or short-term. The **Family Explorer** is the only handbook catering to families on the move in the Emirates. Specifically created for families with children between the ages of 0-14, the **Family Explorer** is written by parents and long-term residents of the UAE. Covering both Dubai and Abu Dhabi, it follows the easy-to-use, reader friendly format of the Explorer Series of guidebooks.

Zappy Explorer (Dubai)

A complete step-by-step guide for getting things done, the Zappy Explorer leads you through all the procedures involved in settling into life, home or business in Dubai – in a zap!

This authoritative step-by-step guide contains over 100 easy to follow procedures on all aspects of life, whether business or personal. It explains in detail how to apply for permits and renew or cancel various government services, while making sense of Dubai's many rules and regulations. Whether you need to apply for a Dubai driving licence, sponsor your family, obtain an Internet connection, or want to set up a free zone company, the **Zappy Explorer** will give you a clear and concise listing of documents required, together with costs, timings, tips and advice (the latest e-government initiative is covered as well).

Images of Dubai & the UAE

A stunning collection of images of Dubai and the UAE as seen through the eyes of a team of local professional photographers.

Images of Dubai is a visual showcase, sharing the secrets of this remarkable land and introducing newcomers to the wonders of Dubai and the United Arab Emirates. Journey with our team of photographers along golden beaches under a pastel sunset, or deep into the mesmerising sands of the desert. View architectural details that make the UAE one of the most visually thrilling urban environments in the world, and dive undersea to encounter the reef creatures who live there. Join us in marvelling at the diversity of astounding locations throughout the seven emirates.

A to Z Explorer (Dubai)

The first and only comprehensive A-Z street guide to Dubai that's quick and easy to use.

At last! A fully cross-referenced, indexed street atlas (110 map pages at 1:15,000 scale) to Dubai that fits in your glove box. This is the book all of Dubai has been waiting for. With concise street names and street numbers cross-referenced with a comprehensive A-Z index of landmarks, places of interest and tourist attractions, this is the only map you will ever need. The **A-Z Explorer** is a unique publication that is set to become the standard tool for navigating around this growing city.

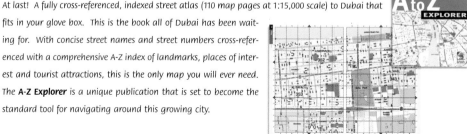

Web Updates

A tremendous amount of research, effort, and passion go into making our guidebooks. However, in this dynamic and fast-paced environment, decisions are swiftly taken and quickly implemented. As your loyal publisher, we will try to provide you with the most current updates on those dives which have DRAMATICALLY changed.

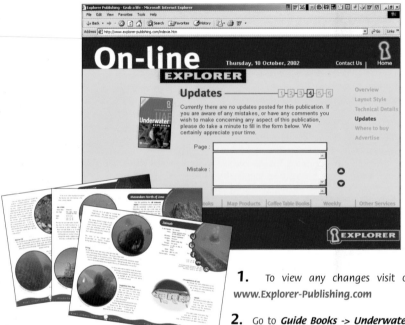

1. To view any changes visit our website **www.Explorer-Publishing.com**

2. Go to *Guide Books -> Underwater Explorer -> Updates* and see whether there are any updates for the dive site you are interested in.

3. All updates are in Adobe PDF format*. You may print in colour or black & white and update your guidebook immediately.

4. If you are aware of any mistakes, or have any comments concerning any aspect of this publication, please fill in our online reader response form... We certainly appreciate your time and feedback.

*If you do not have Adobe Reader, free reader versions may be downloaded from (www.adobe.com) or use the link from our website.

The Leading Annual Lifestyle Guidebook to Dubai

Comprehensive, fun and easy to use, this book covers everything worth knowing about Dubai and where to do it. Meticulously updated annually, this is the most in-depth, practical and accurate coverage of Dubai.
This insiders' guide to what's hot and what's not in Dubai is ideal for residents, short-term visitors, business people and tourists. The **Dubai Explorer** is an essential resource for anyone exploring this vibrant and surprising city.

- General information & UAE overview
- Resident tips & advice
- New, informative business section
- 450 independent restaurant, bar & cafe reviews
- Exploring – museums, heritage, parks & beaches
- Shopping – what to buy & where to buy it
- Activities – sports, leisure, clubs, & kids
- 30 fully referenced photographic maps + a pull-out city map

Available from leading bookstores, hotels, supermarkets, or directly from Explorer Publishing

Explorer Publishing & Distribution • Dubai Media City • Building 2 • Office 502 • PO Box 34275 • Dubai • UAE

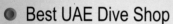

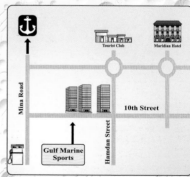

Emirates Diving Association (EDA)

جمـعيــة الإمــارات للغــوص

www.emiratesdiving.com

Emirates Diving Association

EDA was initiated in 1995 by the instructions of
H.H. Sheikh Zayed Bin Sultan Al Nahyan, President of the
United Arab Emirates, who felt the importance
of diving & the need to protect the U.A.E. marine life from
further destruction and pollution.

The main aim of (EDA) is to conserve, protect & restore
the U.A.E. marine resources by understanding and promoting
the marine environment and environmental diving.

Dubai, U.A.E. - P.O. Box: 33220 Tel: +(971 4) 3939390 Fax: +(971 4) 3939391
E-mail: edadiver@emirates.net.ae

NIKONOS-V

Underwater Photographic System

Welcome to a bounty of treasures beneath the waves.

After months of planning, you have finally arrived. Anticipation builds in the incredibly clear underwater environment as you are drawn toward the drop-off. A sheer, vertical wall of intricate coral formations intrigues you, and you ask yourself, can I bring these wondrous sights back?

Yes, you can - with a Nikonos underwater system. When it comes to capturing the beauty of the underwater world, the choice has been Nikonos for over 30 years. The Nikonos range of underwater photographic tools is unrivaled.

The Nikonos-V is rugged, compact , and easy to handle in fast-changing situations. It's the perfect camera for beginners, as well as for professionals who demand quality and reliability. Its system offers the unequaled power of preserving spectacular beauty under water on film for perfect memories.

Nikon

Diving in the UAE

West Coast

Abu Dhabi - Jebel Ali Dive Sites

1. Hammour Barge
2. Jasim
3. Jazirat Sir Bu Na'air
4. Lion City
5. MV Hannan
6. MV Ludwig

Dubai - Umm Al Quwain Dive Sites

7. Anchor Barge
8. Barracuda Barge
9. Car Barge & Tug
10. Cement Barge (Alamina)
11. DB1/SMB
12. Energy Determination
13. Hopper Barge 6 (HB6)
14. Jaramac V
15. Jumeirah Artificial Reef
16. MV Dara
17. MV Sarraf Three
18. Nasteran
19. Neptune 6
20. Rashid Wrecks
21. Zainab

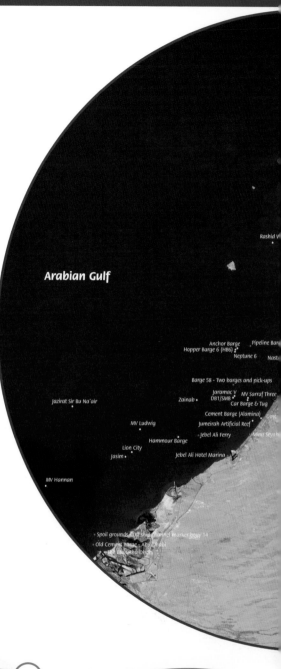

Arabian Gulf

Rashid V

Anchor Barge   Pipeline Bar
Hopper Barge 6 (HB6)
Neptune 6   Nast

Barge 58 - Two barges and pick-ups

Jaramac V   MV Sarraf Three
Zainab •   DB1/SMB •
Car Barge & Tug

Cement Barge (Alamina)

Jazirat Sir Bu Na'air •   Jumeirah Artificial Reef •   Dist

MV Ludwig •   • Jebel Ali Ferry   Mina Seyahi

Hammour Barge   Jumeirah Artificial Reef

Lion City •

Jasim •   Jebel Ali Hotel Marina •

MV Hannan •

• Spoil grounds • Off ship channel marker buoy 14
• Old Cement Barge - Abu Dhabi
• The club Abu Dhabi

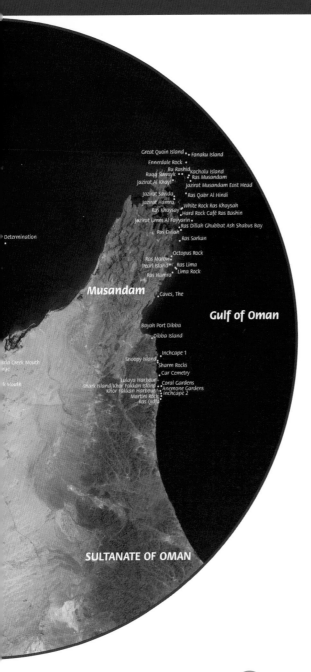

Musandam Peninsula

22. The Caves
23. Lima Rock
24. Octopus Rock
25. Pearl Island
26. Ras Hamra
27. Ras Lima
28. Ras Marovi
29. Musandam North of Lima

East Coast

30. Anemone Gardens
31. Car Cemetery
32. Coral Gardens
33. Dibba Island
34. Inchcape 1
35. Inchcape 2
36. Martini Rock
37. Ras Qidfa
38. Shark Island
39. Sharm Rocks
40. Snoopy Island

● Harbours
○ Dive sites (Covered)
● Dive sites (not covered)

There are certain things every dive centre should have
But there's only one centre that offers more...

Daily East Coast charters

Five star service on every charter

PADI®

Complete range of PADI diver education courses with personalised schedule arrangements, no minimum number requirements and no cut corners

Exclusive dive charters onboard the luxury Princess 20m yacht in conjunction with Yacht Solutions

SCUBA INTERNATIONAL
DIVING COLLEGE
FUJAIRAH

The only registered diving college in the region

Hyperbaric recompression facility on-site with 24 hour on-call doctors. Direct line to the Wirral Hyperbaric Centre and DAN (Divers Alert Network)

Hyperbaric Chamber Operator courses and Diver Medic Training (HSE approved)

Favourable rates at all nearby hotels

TecRec®
DSAT

PADI/DSAT Tec Rec Courses from Discover Tect to Tec Deep Instructor

Over 25 different diver specialty courses available

Visa, transfers and hotel arrangements

Resident PADI Course Director training instructors since 1991

Year round instructor specialty training in over 15 specialty areas

Highly qualified and continually trained instructors

TECHNICAL DIVING INTERNATIONAL

TDI course up to Advanced Trimix instructor

Year-round PADI instructor level courses

Pleasure dives for technically qualified divers to sites between 45 – 115 metres

mares®
just add water

Year-round MARES certified technician courses

Internship programmes from complete novice or non-diver to instructor

Post IDC support from resident Course Director and IDC staff

EMERGENCY
first response

Emergency First Response Instructor training (from Feb '03)

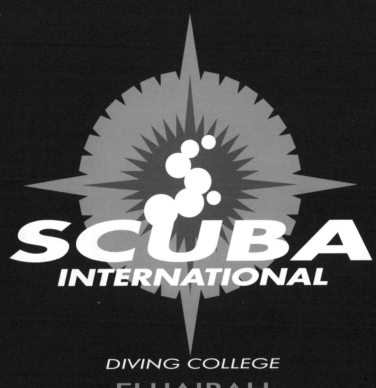

DIVING COLLEGE
FUJAIRAH

SCUBA
INTERNATIONAL
DIVE OPERATIONS

There's only one way to get wet

Underwater Explorer

Diving in the UAE is very special; the lower Arabian Gulf and the Gulf of Oman offer a range of diving and snorkelling to satisfy all tastes and levels of experience. You can choose from over thirty wrecks in relatively shallow water, tropical coral reefs and dramatic coastlines that are virtually undived. These are bathed in year round warm water. Water temperatures range from a cooler 20°C in January to a warmer 35°C in July and August. Although the land temperatures can be in the high 40's in the summer months, it is rarely too hot when out at sea or dipping into the water. Rain usually falls in the early months of the year, January - March, but it is infrequent and never lasts for long.

Areas to Dive

We have divided the region into three main diving areas; the West Coast (lower Arabian Gulf), the Musandam and the East Coast (on the Gulf of Oman and the Indian Ocean side of the peninsular).

Modern highways connect the coasts of the UAE. From the Northern Emirates, the journey from the West to the East Coast is a two hour drive, passing through rolling sand dunes, gravel plains and oasis towns, before crossing the rugged western Hajar Mountains and down to the palm covered coastal strip of the East Coast. Development here is not as advanced as elsewhere in the UAE, offering only a sprinkling of hotels and holiday resorts. In sharp contrast, the West Coast has seen a huge amount of development in the last 25 years, especially in Abu Dhabi and Dubai. Numerous hotels, including plenty of a luxury five-star standard, offer all the facilities a tourist can reasonably expect, and much more.

The weather on the East Coast can be very different to the western UAE. On the Gulf of Oman it is slightly cooler in the summer and there may occasionally be rain in late July and August. The weather will often be calm on this coast, while the West Coast is being buffeted by a 'shamal' (moderate northerly winds). If your dive on one coast is cancelled because of rough seas or high winds, the weather will probably be fine on the other coast. The Musandam is the area to the north of the UAE at the very tip of the peninsular, and is actually part of the Sultanate of Oman. This mountainous region is very beautiful and virtually undeveloped. Its remoteness and lack of access means it is one of the least explored diving areas in the world. Only one paved road runs north from Ras Al Khaimah in the UAE, to Khasab, capital of the Musandam, and many of the small fishing villages along the coast are only accessible by boat or off-road tracks. The hotels are located in Khasab.

Diving

There are many excellent diving organisations and clubs operating in the area that will help you enjoy the wonderful diving. For the Underwater Explorer we have covered as many dive sites as possible with the aim of giving a good representation of the best known and most popular locations. Since most visitors to the UAE are based in Dubai, we have included a large number of West Coast dive sites. These have been divided into two areas; from Abu Dhabi to Jebel Ali and from Jebel Ali to Umm Al Quwain.

Only a few dive sites are safely accessible from the shore, so plan on using a boat. If you have your own boat, there are many slipways available and we have included maps and GPS co-ordinates of the best ones. There are also several first class marinas where you can permanently moor your boat (for a fee!).

Diver Certification

If you are a certified diver, always remember to pack your certification card – without it no dive organisation in the UAE will allow you to dive.

Learning to dive or advancing your existing qualifications with an internationally recognised organisation is very easy to accomplish in the UAE. This can be arranged through one of the many excellent dive centres. Refer to the Dive Directory for contact information.

Good for snorkelling (Yes/No)

 Night dive (Yes/No)

 Charted depth of the dive site in metres

GPS Co-ordinates of the dive sites in degrees, minutes and seconds

 Distance and bearing from the nearest harbours and other dive sites (including reciprocal bearings)

Charted Depth

This is the depth given on charts of the minimum amount of water you will find over wreck sites, underwater obstructions, to the seabed or at the lowest possible tide. However, the actual amount of water covering a site varies, and so the charted depth will occasionally differ from the depth given in the text for individual dive sites.

Levels of Experience

The dive sites described in this book are chosen to suit all levels of diving experience. *Energy Determination* and the *Musandam* are more challenging and require additional precautions to be safely dived. They are recommended only for more experienced divers. For all the other dive sites described, we advise you to take the usual precautions and gauge conditions at the time of your dive.

Skin Protection

A variety of wet suits, 1, 2, 3 and 5mm, dive skins (Lycra suits), and/or coveralls offer protection against cold thermoclines, hydrocorals, jellyfish stings, sunstroke and heatstroke.

Water Temperature

Water temperatures in °C throughout the year in the southern Arabian Gulf:

January	February	March	April	May	June	July
18-23	20-23	20-25	24-26	27-30	27-32	31-35

August	September	October	November	December
33-36	30-33	30-33	25-30	23-25

Water temperatures in °C throughout the year for the East Coast and Musandam. (Note that these temperatures are difficult to predict due to thermoclines, which result from cold water flowing in from the Indian Ocean.)

January	February	March	April	May	June	July
21-23	20-23	20-24	22-24	22-27	23-27	28-30

August	September	October	November	December
32-30	31-29	30-27	29-26	26-23

Marine Life Table

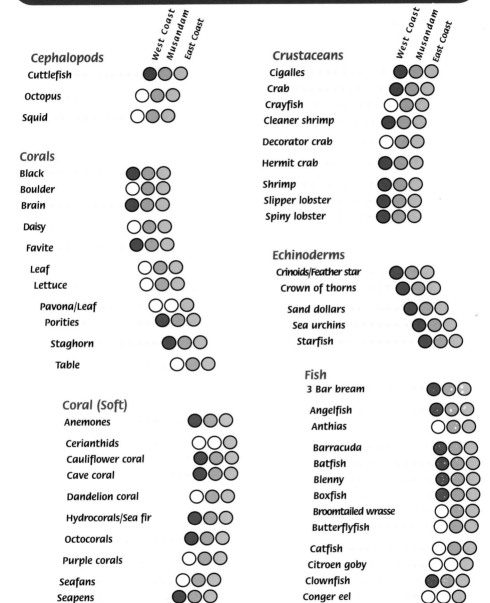

Cephalopods	West Coast	Musandam	East Coast
Cuttlefish			
Octopus			
Squid			

Corals

	West Coast	Musandam	East Coast
Black			
Boulder			
Brain			
Daisy			
Favite			
Leaf			
Lettuce			
Pavona/Leaf			
Porites			
Staghorn			
Table			

Coral (Soft)

	West Coast	Musandam	East Coast
Anemones			
Cerianthids			
Cauliflower coral			
Cave coral			
Dandelion coral			
Hydrocorals/Sea fir			
Octocorals			
Purple corals			
Seafans			
Seapens			
Teddybear			
Whip corals			

Crustaceans	West Coast	Musandam	East Coast
Cigalles			
Crab			
Crayfish			
Cleaner shrimp			
Decorator crab			
Hermit crab			
Shrimp			
Slipper lobster			
Spiny lobster			

Echinoderms

	West Coast	Musandam	East Coast
Crinoids/Feather star			
Crown of thorns			
Sand dollars			
Sea urchins			
Starfish			

Fish

	West Coast	Musandam	East Coast
3 Bar bream			
Angelfish			
Anthias			
Barracuda			
Batfish			
Blenny			
Boxfish			
Broomtailed wrasse			
Butterflyfish			
Catfish			
Citroen goby			
Clownfish			
Conger eel			
Cornetfish			
Crocodilefish			

Marine Life Table

	West Coast	Musandam	East Coast
Cowfish	○	○	○
Damselfish	○	◐	◐
Diamond trevally	●	○	○
Dottyback	●	○	◐
Emperor/Angelfish	○	○	○
Flounder	○	○	◐
Frogfish	○	○	◐
Fusilier	●	●	◐
Goatfish	●	◐	◐
Goby	●	●	◐
Grouper	●	○	◐
Halibut	○	○	◐
Hammour	●	◐	◐
Hawkfish	○	○	◐
Honeycomb moray	○	◐	◐
Jawfish (hole goby)	○	○	○
Jack/Tuna	●	◐	◐
Kingfish	○	○	◐
Lionfish	●	◐	◐
Mackerel	●	○	◐
Moses sole	○	○	◐
Moray eels	●	◐	◐
Mullet	○	◐	◐
Oceanic triggerfish	●	○	◐
Parrotfish	●	◐	◐
Pennantfish	●	◐	◐
Picasso triggerfish	○	○	◐
Pipefish	◐	◐	◐
Pufferfish	●	◐	◐
Pygmy seamoth	○	○	○
Queenfish	○	◐	◐
Rabbitfish (shrimpfish)	●	○	○
Red big-eye	○	○	◐
Remora	○	○	◐
Robust pipefish	○	○	◐
Sergeant major	●	○	◐
Scorpion fish	●	○	◐
Sea horse	●	○	◐
Snapper	●	◐	◐
Sohal	●	○	◐
Squirrelfish	●	○	◐
Stone fish	●	○	◐
Striped eel catfish	○	○	◐
Sunfish	○	○	◐
Surgeonfish	●	◐	◐
Sweetlips	●	◐	◐
Tobyfish	○	○	◐
Trevally	●	◐	◐

Other

	West Coast	Musandam	East Coast
Dolphins	●	◐	◐
Jellyfish	●	◐	◐
Sea snake	●	○	◐
Sea squirts	●	◐	◐
Turtles	●	◐	◐

Sharks & Rays

	West Coast	Musandam	East Coast
Bell ray	●	◐	◐
Blacktip reef shark	●	◐	◐
Blind Juvenile shark	●	◐	◐
Bull shark	○	◐	◐
Eagle ray	●	○	◐
Electric/Torpedo ray	●	◐	◐
Feather-tailed ray	●	◐	◐

Marine Life Table

	West Coast	Musandam	East Coast
Grey reef shark	○	●	○
Guitar/Shovelnose ray	●	●	●
Hammerhead shark	○	●	●
Leopard ray	●	●	○
Leopard shark	●	●	●
Manta/Devil ray	○	●	●
Marble ray	●	●	●
Nurse shark	○	●	○
Shark eggs	○	●	●
Sting ray	●	●	●
Whaleshark	●	●	○
Whitetip shark	○	●	○
Zebra shark	○	●	○

Shells / Worms

	West Coast	Musandam	East Coast
Cone shells	○	●	●
Cowrie shells	●	●	●
Fanworms	●	●	●
Featherworm	●	●	●
Flatworms	●	●	●
Murex shell	●	●	●
Nudibranchs	●	●	●
Pearl oyster	●	●	●
Sea hares	●	○	●
Thorny oyster-shell	●	●	●

Sponges

	West Coast	Musandam	East Coast
	●	●	●

13

West Coast Dives

Arabian Gulf

Ras Al Khaimah

Dubai

Fujairah

Abu Dhabi UAE

Hatta

Al Ain

OMAN

Gulf of Oman

MV Dara

Anchor Barge

Pipeline Barge

Hopper Barge 6 (HB6)

Hamria Creek Mouth

Neptune 6

Nasteran

Barracuda Barge

Sharjah Creek Mouth

Barge 58 - Two barges and pick-ups

Jaramac V

MV Sarraf Three

Jazirat Sir Bu Na'air

Zainab

DB1/SMB

Car Barge & Tug

Dubai Creek Mouth

Cement Barge (Alamina)

Dosc Harbour

MV Ludwig

Jumeirah Artificial Reef

Hammour Barge

Jebel Ali Ferry

Mina Seyahi Harbour (DIMC)

Lion City

Jasim

Jebel Ali Hotel Marina

MV Hannan

Abu Dhabi Area

Spoil grounds - Off ship channel marker bouy 14

Old Cement Barge - Abu Dhabi

The Club Abu Dhabi

● Harbours

● Dive sites (Covered)

● Dive sites (not covered)

16

Diving the West Coast

Arabian angelfish

The West Coast is a wreck diver's paradise, with wrecks dating back to the early sixties to choose from, all of which can only be accessed by boat. The wrecks are generally the most interesting places to dive, since they attract a plethora of marine life.

At 984 km long, the Arabian Gulf is a shallow extension of the Indian Ocean, and offers a sandy, almost flat, featureless seabed with a few isolated coral reefs. Its narrowest point is at the Strait of Hormuz (the northern tip of the Peninsula), where it is 56 km wide. The average depth along the UAE coast is 30 metres, increasing to over 100 metres through the Strait of Hormuz.

The tidal movement is slight, with the currents only becoming stronger during spring tides and around the full moon. With a few exceptions, the currents have little effect on most of the dives. Visibility ranges between 5-15 metres, although there are exceptional days when it reaches 20 metres plus. Most of the wrecks are within a 30 minute boat journey of the shore.

Sleeping parrotfish

Night Diving

Night diving on the West Coast is spectacular; until you have dived with a powerful light at night and seen all the colours, you won't know what you have missed! The wrecks, which appear orange and muddy brown during the day, turn into rainbows of colour at night and a whole new set of marine residents appear to feed and forage.

The wrecks offer such a small area of sanctuary for the fish that they have to

17

hide in every available hole, crevice and corner. As a diver this means that you can get very close to a wide variety of resting fish.

At night, sites like the *DB1* and *Car Barge* are always special and memorable. With the exception of the *Jasim*, *Lion City* and *MV Ludwig* we have dived all the sites covered in this book at night, even including the *Energy Determination*.

When returning from the more distant sites everyone tends to want to get home as quickly as possible, however, beware! On a journey home at night from the *Energy Determination*, we ran into unmarked fishing nets. The nets jammed around the propellers, immobilising the boats. Unfortunately, the waters off the coast of the UAE sometimes have the odd piece of semi-submerged drifting debris. This can be difficult to spot and easily run into at night.

Diver Safety

To make your wreck dives safe and pleasant, keep in mind the following points:

- Wear protective clothing. The wreck's surface may be covered with stinging hydrocorals and protruding pieces of jagged metal.
- If it is your first time on the site and you do not have a dive guide, do not enter the wreck unless a large exit point is visible through the other side.
- Be extra careful if you are diving a wreck after a storm; it may have become unstable or fragile.
- Do not enter a wreck without appropriate training.
- If you intend to penetrate a wreck, use a rope or guideline – tie it to the outside of the wreck to help you find your way out.
- Take a torch/light.
- Once inside the wreck be cautious, as wrecks tend to silt up quickly. Control your finning techniques to minimise this effect.

Ships Weights & Measures

- 35 cubic feet of salt water weighs 1 ton
- 36 cubic feet of fresh water weighs 1 ton
- 1 cubic foot = 0.0283 cubic metres
- 1 cubic metre = 35.31 cubic feet
- 1 ton = 2,240 lbs or 1,000 kilograms
- 1 tonne = 1,000 kilograms

Displacement Tonnage

This is the weight of water displaced by the boat. It is equal to the weight of the boat and all that is in her; therefore, it varies with her draft. Displacement in tons = volume of water displaced (in cubic feet) divided by 35 or 36 (depending on whether the water is salt or fresh respectively). Displacement may also be quoted in tons.

Dead-weight (DWT)

This is the weight in tons of 2,240 lbs, 1 tonne, or 1,000 kilograms of cargo, stores, fuel, passengers and crew carried by the boat when loaded to her maximum summer load line.

Gross Tonnage

The gross tonnage is measured according to the law of the national authority with which the boat is registered. This measurement is, broadly, the capacity in cubic feet of all spaces within the hull and enclosed spaces above the deck available for cargo, stores, passengers and crew (with certain exceptions), and divided by 100.

Net Tonnage

This is derived from the gross tonnage by deducting the space used for the accommodation of the crew, navigation equipment, machinery and fuel.

Builder's Measure

Until 1873, the tonnage of a vessel was called Builders Measurement (BM). This was more than likely based on the number of casks the vessel could carry. After 1873, displacement tonnage was used, and from about 1926 onwards, the actual weight has been calibrated. Data on some vessels is shown in BM, but over time this number has been converted to actual tons, and may not be precise, i.e. a vessel shown as 100BM is not automatically 100 tons.

Wreck Data

Under each dive site, we have used the following layout to provide as much information as possible on the wreck. This has been obtained from either the Lloyds Register of Shipping or from the Hydrographic List.

Wreck Register   The number allocated by Lloyds or the Hydrographic Society.

Name   The original name of the vessel when built.

Nationality   Details of which country/flag the boat was sailing under.

Year Built   The year the vessel was built.

Type   Cargo Vessels, Coastal Barges, Coastal Tankers, Coastal Vessels, Landing Crafts, Motor Lighter, Passenger Liners, Tugs, Very Large Crude Container (VLCC).

Tonnage   Refer to information on Ship Weights & Measures.

Dimensions

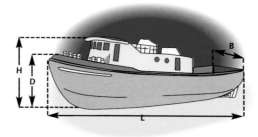

Length (L) – Length from stern to bow.
Breadth (B) – Beam from port to starboard.
Depth (D) – Depth from deck to keel.
Height (H) – Height from keel to the top of the bridge.

Cargo   What the boat was carrying at the time of loss.

Date Sunk   The date the vessel was sunk

Charted Depth   As per the Admiralty chart information based on the lowest astronomical tide (LAT).

Depth   Depth where the wreckage lies

Hammour Barge

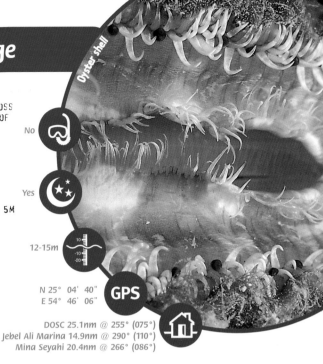

Oyster Shell

WRECK REGISTER: 108301272

NAME:	UNKNOWN AT TIME OF LOSS [SEE CIRCUMSTANCES OF LOSS]
NATIONALITY:	UNKNOWN
YEAR BUILT:	UNKNOWN
TYPE:	OPEN HOLD BARGE
TONNAGE:	860 TONS GROSS
DIMENSIONS:	L: 60M, B: 10M, D: 5M
CARGO:	PIPES
DATE SUNK:	UNKNOWN
CHARTED DEPTH:	12–15 METRES

No

Yes

12-15m

N 25° 04' 40"
E 54° 46' 06"   **GPS**

DOSC 25.1nm @ 255° (075°)
Jebel Ali Marina 14.9nm @ 290° (110°)
Mina Seyahi 20.4nm @ 266° (086°)

Circumstances of Loss

Sunk by a local fisherman to form an artificial offshore reef.

Details

The vessel lies upright in 12-15 metres of water. Her hold contains a cargo of pipes, making a perfect home for hammour, which is how the vessel obtained her name. The wheelhouse is in place, but all the 'goodies' have been removed. It is not known when this wreck was sunk, but judging by the marine growth, it has been resting on the seabed for at least 15 years.

Diving

This is a relatively small wreck with a few pieces of debris lying on the sand nearby. Our suggested dive plan is to start at the base of the wreck and swim around it looking on the sand and in the debris. Then inspect the hull of the barge where it rests on the seabed, since this is where many of the smaller marine residents hide. The small cabin is accessible and worth exploring. Have a look inside the pipes in the hold; you will always find some of the resident hammour hiding there.

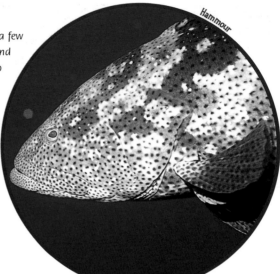

Hammour

Marine Life

The fish life is reasonably tame since the wreck is not often visited by divers. These shallow wrecks are home to the more brightly coloured reef fish like the orange dottyback, and their less colourful cousins, the Gulf dottyback. Look out for one of the several varieties of blennies to be found on this site. It's amazing how these colourful fish manage to squeeze into the tiniest of spaces, even trying to hide inside empty barnacle shells! They can be seen waiting near their little holes or just inside with the top of their head sticking out, ready to dart out of sight at the first sign of danger. Arabian angelfish can be seen all over the wreck, picking over the encrustations. This wreck is also home to moon wrasse.

Blenny

Jasim

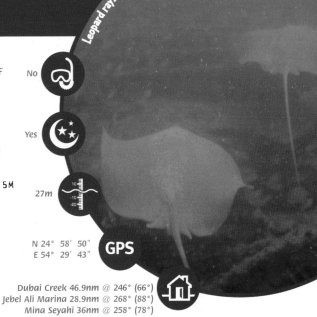

Leopard rays

WRECK REGISTER: 108301272

NAME:	UNKNOWN AT TIME OF LOSS [SEE CIRCUMSTANCES OF LOSS]
NATIONALITY:	UNKNOWN
YEAR BUILT:	UNKNOWN
TYPE:	MV COASTAL TANKER
TONNAGE:	1,200 TONS GROSS
DIMENSIONS:	L: 60M, B: 10M, D: 5M
CARGO:	BALLAST
DATE SUNK:	MARCH 25, 1986
CHARTED DEPTH:	23 METRES

No

Yes

27m

N 24° 58' 50"
E 54° 29' 43"

GPS

Dubai Creek 46.9nm @ 246° (66°)
Jebel Ali Marina 28.9nm @ 268° (88°)
Mina Seyahi 36nm @ 258° (78°)

Circumstances of Loss

The UAE armed forces used the vessel for target practice.

Details

Resting on her port side, the Jasim lies in 26-27 metres of water and is broken into three large sections. The stern section consists of the engine room and accommodation, with the large single propeller and rudder still in place. The middle cargo section is a tangled, confused collection of broken hatches, rigging and old vehicle parts and lorry wheels. The bow section is more or less intact with lamp rooms and deck winches.

Diving

This site is always an interesting dive, although care must be taken as the average depth is 27 metres. Watch your bottom time and allow plenty of air for safety stops.

The bridge and living quarters can be accessed through several hatches. The engine room is a little more difficult to enter, although access can be gained through two deck hatches aft of the accommodation area. Once inside, care should be taken as the engine room is very silted.

Three bar bream

Marine Life

This wreck offers the opportunity to see some unusual marine life, and there are several species of brittle stars and cowrie shells. The shells are normally nocturnal, but on this site you can usually find one or two during the day.

Although this wreck was sunk 15 years ago, the marine growth is not as advanced as on other wrecks such as *DB1*. Hydrocorals, orange sponges and sea squirts are predominant.

Cowrie shell

Jazirat Sir Bu Na'air

Turtle

NAME: JAZIRAT SIR BU NA'AIR

LOCATION: 70 KM OFFSHORE BETWEEN DUBAI AND ABU DHABI

DIVE SITE: CORAL REEFS, SHELVING SANDY BOTTOM AND DROP-OFFS

CHARTED DEPTH: UP TO 36 METRES

Yes

Yes

36m

N 25° 13' 30"
E 54° 13' 00"

GPS

Dubai Creek 58.7nm @ 266° (86°)
Jebel Ali Marina 46.3nm @ 286° (106°)
Mina Seyahi 51.1nm @ 278° (98°)

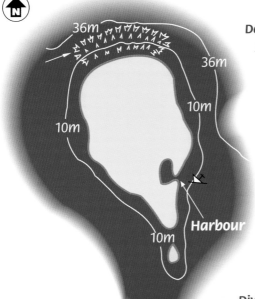

36m
36m
10m
10m
10m

Harbour

Details

Jazirat Sir Bu Na'air is an island off the Gulf coast of the Emirates. It is just over 1 km long by 0.5 km wide and is used by the UAE as a military outpost and coastguard station. There are no restrictions on sailing or diving near the island, but as it is a sensitive military base, it is advisable not to land. That said, you do occasionally see people picnicking on the beaches.

Diving

Towards the northern end of the island there is a large area of table and staghorn coral in magnificent condition. The coral runs north to the 20 metre mark, then the seabed shelves down to 30 metres plus. The north-eastern side has large flat rocks and coral, and there are more extensive areas of coral to the north-west. Off the southern tip of the island, the sandy bottom runs to 20 metres, ending with a small sea mount. At the entrance to the harbour on the south-east side, there is a partially submerged barge wreck. Although a long journey, diving at *Jazirat Sir Bu Na'air* is definitely well worth it.

Barracuda

Marine Life

The island is rarely visited by divers or fishermen and the resulting lack of disturbance encourages prolific shoals of fish. There are numerous large pelagic fish, spotted eagle rays, barracuda and large rays.

Snorkelling

This is a great place for snorkelling, especially on the northern coral field, which starts at 5 metres and gently runs down into deeper water. The visibility is good, and as it is one of the protected turtle breeding areas, turtles are frequently seen by snorkellers. By using a snorkel, you don't scare the marine life with the noise of your breathing in the way that divers do.

Environment

HH Dr Sheikh Sultan bin Mohammed Al Qassimi, Supreme Council Member and Ruler of Sharjah, issued Administrative Order No. 3 for the year 2000, banning all activities considered harmful to the environment of *Jazirat Sir Bu Na'air* island.

The six article order seeks to halt the deterioration of the island's environment, protect its marine resources and life, and develop its natural resources. The order bans the fishing of all species of sea turtle, collection of their eggs or damage of their nesting beaches along the island's coastline. The order also bans any activities that could possibly threaten the safety of resident or migrating birds on the island.

Manta ray

Lion City

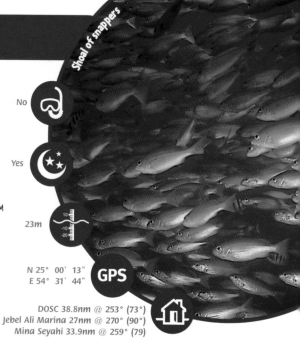

Shoal of snappers

WRECK REGISTER: 108300171

NAME:	UNKNOWN AT TIME OF LOSS [SEE CIRCUMSTANCES OF LOSS]
NATIONALITY:	UNKNOWN
YEAR BUILT:	UNKNOWN
TYPE:	MV COASTAL TANKER
TONNAGE:	1200 GROSS
DIMENSIONS:	L: 60M, B: 10M, D: 5M
CARGO:	BALLAST
DATE SUNK:	MAY 1, 1986
CHARTED DEPTH:	23 METRES

No

Yes

23m

N 25° 00' 13"
E 54° 31' 44"

GPS

DOSC 38.8nm @ 253° (73°)
Jebel Ali Marina 27nm @ 270° (90°)
Mina Seyahi 33.9nm @ 259° (79)

Circumstances of Loss

The UAE armed forces used the vessel for target practice.

Details

The vessel lies on its port side in 30 metres of water with its bow facing 300°. It is basically intact with the funnel and some rigging lying on the sand. The original name, *Lion City*, is clearly visible on the bow, and there is also a star emblem on the funnel.

28

Diving

The living quarters and engine rooms are easily accessed without much difficulty. If you do want to enter and investigate the interior, remember that the wreck is lying on its side, so you will have to think about where you are going. Swimming along stairways that don't go up or down and arriving in rooms on their side can be disorientating. Look at the shape of holes and decide which is the easiest way for you to fit through. Don't forget that with your tank and jacket you are now deeper than you are wide. If you feel yourself becoming stuck, always go back before you really do get stuck!

Aeolid nudibranch

On the deck, the oil transfer pipes run almost from the bridge to the bosun's storerooms forward, covering most of the available deck space. This is an interesting area to search for unusual marine life.

Marine Life

The marine growth is not as advanced as on other wrecks, although recently some white coral patches on the deck and on the upper side of the hull have begun to form. Covering large areas of the hull, these corals are in circular patches of about 100 mm across. The sea firs have given the hull a dull light brown colour. On one of the walkways across the pipes, a colony of white soft corals is forming on the treads and handrails. Shoals of yellow coloured blackspot snapper swim over and under the labyrinth of pipes on the deck hunting for their quarry. These little hunters are distinctively coloured with a black spot under the dorsal fins and longitudinal yellow pinstripes. Working in packs they chase their prey or wait alone in the shadows for dinner to come to them.

The distance from the shore makes this wreck a good second dive after exploring either the *Jasim* or the *MV Ludwig*.

Shoal of black spot snapper

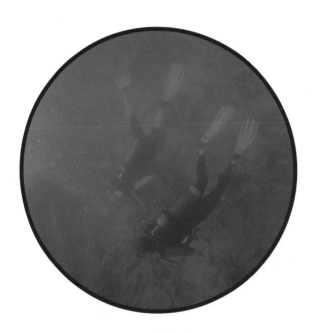

MV Hannan

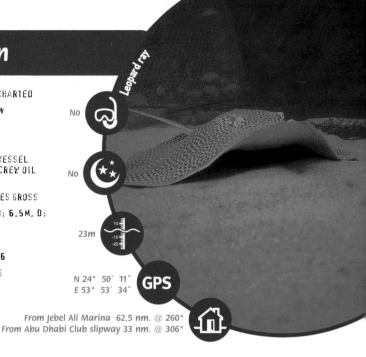

WRECK REGISTER: NOT CHARTED

NAME: *MV HANNAN*

NATIONALITY: UNKNOWN

YEAR BUILT: UNKNOWN

TYPE: COASTAL VESSEL SINGLE SCREW OIL ENGINE

TONNAGE: 288-TONNES GROSS

DIMENSIONS: L: 42M, B: 6.5M, D: 2.6M

CARGO: NONE

DATE SUNK: 3 AUG 1986

CHARTED DEPTH: 20 METRES

Leopard ray

No

No

23m

N 24° 50' 11"
E 53° 53' 34"

GPS

From Jebel Ali Marina 62.5 nm. @ 260°
From Abu Dhabi Club slipway 33 nm. @ 306°

Circumstances of Loss

Unknown, probably sank while working in the Abu Dhabi oil fields as the position is very close to offshore rigs and platforms.

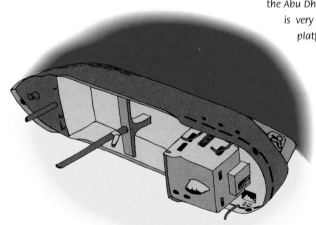

Diving

This is a small coastal vessel, her stern roughly pointing towards the north, marked by two buoys: the official cardinal wreck buoy and the other one is a huge barrel with a large chain link anchored less than three meters from the stern on the starboard side.

Once you have descended, go around the wreck in a clockwise direction. Starting from the seabed, go along the wreck to the bow. Ascend a little in order to explore the hold area separated by a small derrick splitting the hold into two and perhaps try some wreck penetration. It is possible to access the bridge and accommodation areas via a small window and also via the companionway door. If you go through the door and out of the top small window of the wheelhouse you will find a small box looking like a left-over treasure box!

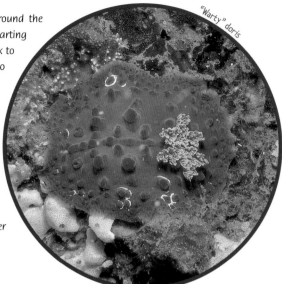

"Warty" doris

Marine Life

This site attracts very large shoals of fish. The currents cause the fish to congregate on this wreck in shoals and you will see various species of jacks, yellow striped jacks and "finger jacks" also known as "queenfish". The shoals share the currents with large, mean looking barracuda, some of which have unusual barred markings.

The site is also home to some very big hammour, more than 1m long, large puffers, batfish and huge rays, regular bell rays as well as the usual leopard ray. It is not uncommon to see guitarsharks, eagle rays and electric rays. The rays are sometimes seen on the upper surfaces of the hull and companionways. Look for nudibranchs which often cling to the hull and you may be lucky to find one of the largest nudibranchs in the Gulf, going by the nickname of "warty doris", approximately 125mm. Although it is large, it is well camouflaged and easy to overlook.

Diver on the Hannan

32

This site has some unusual life, not seen regularly in the Gulf waters, small colonial ascidians, translucent delicate sea squirts and an unusual type of purple soft coral in clumps all over the wreck.

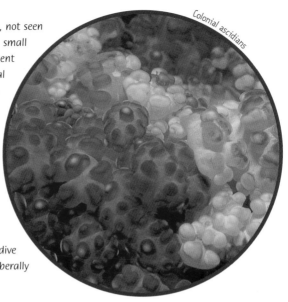

Colonial ascidians

Safety

The currents on this site can be very strong and being located well offshore, assistance may not be immediately available.

You should also be prepared with a dive knife or net cutters as this site is liberally covered with old nets.

Translucent sea squirts

MV Ludwig

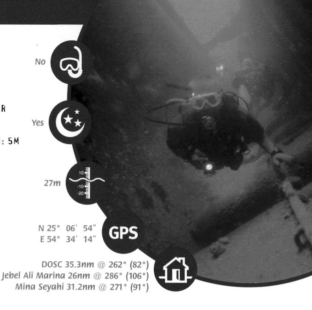

WRECK REGISTER: —
NAME: *MV LUDWIG*
NATIONALITY: UNKNOWN
YEAR BUILT: UNKNOWN
TYPE: MV COASTAL TANKER
TONNAGE: 1200 GROSS
DIMENSIONS: L: 60M, B: 10M, D: 5M
CARGO: BALLAST
DATE SUNK: 2000
CHARTED DEPTH: 27 METRES

No

Yes

27m

N 25° 06' 54"
E 54° 34' 14" **GPS**

DOSC 35.3nm @ 262° (82°)
Jebel Ali Marina 26nm @ 286° (106°)
Mina Seyahi 31.2nm @ 271° (91°)

Circumstances of Loss

The UAE armed forces used the vessel for target practice.

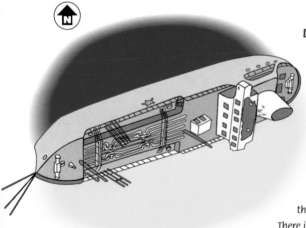

Details

The *MV Ludwig* lies, more or less intact, in 27 metres of water on her port side, with the bow pointing east at 70°. The bridge received a direct hit and the explosion ripped out the internal walls and roof of the bridge. Damage can also be seen on the funnel, where shrapnel from the bridge punched holes in it. There is another projectile exit hole on the starboard side of the hull.

Diving

Exploration inside the wreck is via the bridge section, down into the crew quarters or through the stern hatches into the engine room.

This wreck is very similar to the *Lion City* with the deck a maze of oil transfer pipes and valves. You could almost be fooled into thinking you were diving on the *Lion City*, as both ships were coastal oil tankers and are lying on their port sides. However, the *MV Ludwig* is larger with two bridges over the pipe runs and a small deckhouse forward of the bridge.

Batfish

Marine Life

Marine growth on the *Ludwig* is only just beginning to take hold, with hydrocorals and sea squirts being among the first inhabitants. The wreck's pipes and rigging offer security to a profusion of reef fish, like the shoals of pennantfish that glide over structures in close formation and the damselfish which dart in and out of the cover of the iron and steel. A large resident shoal of yellow snappers seeks security from the hordes of barracuda that constantly circle the wreck, while batfish live further out.

Shoal of yellow snappers

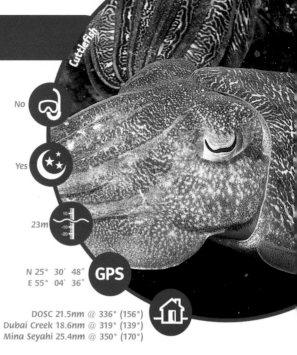

Cuttlefish

WRECK REGISTER: –

NAME:	PONTOON 300 (FORMERLY *THE LEENA*)
NATIONALITY:	UNKNOWN
YEAR BUILT:	UNKNOWN
TYPE:	BARGE
TONNAGE:	3,900 TONS
DIMENSIONS:	L: 82M, B: 27M, D: 5M
CARGO:	BALLAST
DATE SUNK:	APRIL, 1998
CHARTED DEPTH:	23 METRES

No

Yes

23m

N 25° 30' 48"
E 55° 04' 36"   **GPS**

DOSC 21.5nm @ 336° (156°)
Dubai Creek 18.6nm @ 319° (139°)
Mina Seyahi 25.4nm @ 350° (170°)

Circumstances of Loss

Sunk by the White Sea Shipping Company to form an artificial offshore reef.

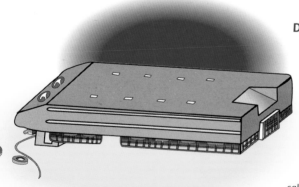

Details

This large wreck lies upside down, resting on the forward machinery cabin in 23-25 metres of water. The cabin contains the anchor winches and the cargo and ballast transfer pumps, with her bulk being supported by the cabin and deck equipment. There is a large open area between the deck and the sand.

Diving

As the vessel is rectangular and slab-sided and the currents quite strong on this site, it can be difficult to anchor. The wreck lies on a ridge of rock almost a metre high, making this one of the few dive sites in the Gulf where the seabed has some features that are worth exploring. You should take a powerful torch/flashlight to search under the hull of the barge, looking up at the overhead deck.

Upturned Anchor Barge

Marine Life

The marine growth is starting to establish itself, with scallops, oysters and small clumps of black sea squirts taking hold, and hydrocorals covering all surfaces and blurring the edges. On the surrounding sand and rocky bottom, flatworms (black with a colourful orange edging) abound in February and March.

Cuttlefish can also be seen on this wreck. These amazing creatures have a neon-like line running around their mantle and they can alter their colour and shape in less than a second. When startled, their body surface becomes goosebump-like and their colour changes to blend in with the surroundings.

Anchor Barge

Barracuda Barge

WRECK REGISTER:	NOT CHARTED
NAME:	ORIGINAL NAME UNKNOWN
NATIONALITY:	UNKNOWN
YEAR BUILT:	UNKNOWN
TYPE:	MV COASTAL BARGE – SINGLE SCREW
TONNAGE:	800 GROSS
DIMENSIONS:	L: 30M B: 10M D: 4M
CARGO:	NONE
DATE SUNK:	UNKNOWN
CHARTED DEPTH:	18 METRES

Wheel House

Yes

No

18m

N 25° 27' 16"
E 55° 22' 41" **GPS**

From Mina Seyahi 25.1nm. @ 30°
From Mina Seyahi 6.4nm. @ 255°

Circumstances of Loss

The circumstances of loss are unknown. As the engine and steering gear have been removed, it is highly likely that it was sunk by a local fisherman to form an artificial reef. In the winter of 1997, a fisherman informed Scuba Arabia of this wreck.

Details

The barge sits upright in 18 meters with the bow facing 340° on a flat, featureless sandy seabed with a few bits of scattered wreckage around the barge. The wheelhouse and engine room are double storeyed, an unusual feature for a barge. There are several windows and doors, giving easy access to the interior. When entering the small rooms be careful not to stir up the silt which reduces the visibility. The top of the wheelhouse is at 10m and covered in algae and shells.

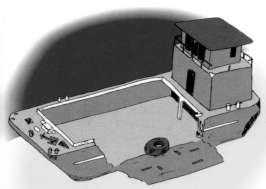

Small shoals of fish congregate around the top of the wheelhouse; these fish are really tame.

The wreck is small and easy to go around several times in one dive. Inspect the outside hull and look for small gobies with shrimp in their sandy homes on the seabed. Then explore the hold before you go in and out of the wheelhouse. Examine the unusual anchor still sitting on the bow.

Barracuda

Marine Life

During the winter months, as the wreck's name suggests, it is surrounded by shoals of barracuda; during the summer months they are not as abundant. When the water becomes too warm they move to cooler, deeper water. The wreck is home to the usual yellow snappers, which carpet the wreck, above it, around it and in it. You will find them squeezed in every little nook and cranny. The cowries on this wreck are a similar rusty-brown colour as the ones found on 'the Dara', from absorbing the iron oxide. The wreck is covered in various types of orange, red, brown and black sponges. There are lots of barnacles with their feathery arms feeding by catching small algae and other tasty things. Several types of nudibranchs inhabit this wreck, their gills pulsing as they breathe; look to see if you can find their eggs in circle patterns close by. The wreck is covered with a white fern-like plant; take care as these are stinging hydroids and may give you a nasty sting or rash.

The Wheelhouse

Snorkelling

Snorkelling: YES, you will be able to see the top of the wheelhouse from the surface.

Car Barge & Tug

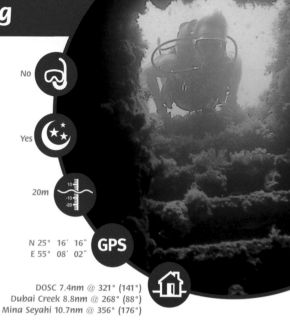

WRECK REGISTER: —

NAME:	UNKNOWN
NATIONALITY:	UNKNOWN
YEAR BUILT:	UNKNOWN
TYPE:	COASTAL BARGE
TONNAGE:	UNKNOWN
DIMENSIONS:	L: 60M, B: 20M, D: 2.6M
CARGO:	OLD VEHICLE PARTS
DATE SUNK:	1986
CHARTED DEPTH:	20 METRES

No

Yes

20m

N 25° 16' 16"
E 55° 08' 02" **GPS**

DOSC 7.4nm @ 321° (141°)
Dubai Creek 8.8nm @ 268° (88°)
Mina Seyahi 10.7nm @ 356° (176°)

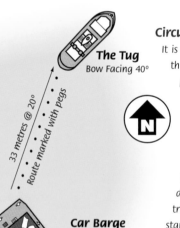

The Tug
Bow Facing 40°

33 metres @ 20°
Route marked with pegs

N

Car Barge
Bow Facing 320°

Circumstances of Loss

It is understood that in 1986 both the barge and tug were bought privately by a local fisherman, towed out and sunk at their present position to form an artificial offshore reef. However, local rumours suggest that the vessels hit stormy weather, the barge found itself in difficulties, and although they tried to off-load some of the cars, it started to sink very quickly, taking the tug with it, since there wasn't enough time to remove the tow rope.

Details

The car barge is virtually intact, less her brass fittings, and lies upright with her bow pointing north-west, at 320°. She has an open hold, filled with old cars and vehicle parts, and a small wheelhouse and cabin on the stern. The depth from the surface to the top of the barge is 15 metres.

At the bow a row of pegs runs for 33 metres from the barge to a small tug, 18.5 metres long and 5 metres wide, which was used for harbour work. The tug sits almost upright on the seabed, but with a slight list to port, and her bow points north-east at a 45° angle.

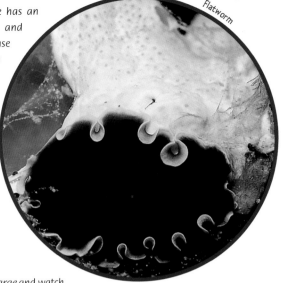

Flatworm

Diving

Make a trip into the cabin on the *Car Barge* and watch the fish pass by the windows outside. The cabin masks the noise of your breathing and hides your bubble trail from the marine life, and you'll find that the larger patrolling fish close in. There are other sections of debris to the north of the barge for the more adventurous to explore. Lying in close proximity to each other, these two wrecks make for a good day and an excellent night dive.

The small tug

Marine Life

The large shoals of yellow coloured snappers and fusiliers that frequent this wreck always make it a pleasure to dive here. If they are not in large shoals, like clouds hugging the upper sections of the wrecks, they are swarming in and out of the wreckage in the hold and cabins.

Although these wrecks have been sunk for 15 years, there is relatively little marine growth. However, hard corals are forming on all the upper surfaces. Sea firs and orange sponges are predominant and you can also find several clumps of white soft coral. Smaller reef fish stay close to the wrecks, while the large predators circle, waiting for an easy meal.

Cement Barge

WRECK REGISTER: 108300778 & LLOYDS WRECK REGISTER NO. 204

NAME: *ALAMINA*

NATIONALITY: IRAQI

YEAR BUILT: UNKNOWN

TYPE: MOTOR LIGHTER, SINGLE SCREW

TONNAGE: GROSS TONNAGE UNKNOWN

DIMENSIONS: L: 25M, B: 7M, D: 7M

CARGO: 1200 TONS OF CEMENT

DATE SUNK: MAY 6, 1971

CHARTED DEPTH: 10 METRES

Yes

Yes

12m

N 25° 10' 20"
E 55° 12' 17"   GPS

Dubai Creek 7.8nm @ 217° (37°)
Mina Seyahi 5.7nm @ 034° (214°)
DOSC 0.7nm @ 257° (77°)

Circumstances of Loss

The vessel was en route for Dubai, but sank in heavy weather.

Details

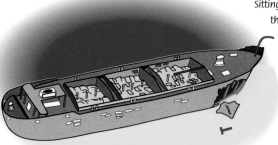

Sitting upright in 12 metres of water, the barge is more or less intact, although in recent years it has started to deteriorate, with large cracks and holes appearing along the hull. The wreck still carries its original cargo of cement and the bags can be clearly seen. The depth from the surface to the top of the superstructure is approximately 5 metres, and the average depth of the deck and holds is 8-10 metres.

Diving

Start your dive on the sandy bottom and swim around the wreck. Look under the stern for hammour and snapper hiding in the depression where the sand has been washed away beneath the propeller shaft. On the port side of the stern lie the remains of the funnel. Moving forward, investigate the numerous holes where the hull rests in the sand. The lower section of the bow has collapsed leaving an opening right through the wreck. All that remains of the bridge and cabin is the framework. The separate holds still contain their cargo of cement bags, but the bulkheads are breaking up; if you use a bright light, you will often find quite large fish resting in the gaps. The hatch cover to the engine room is missing and although the engine room is silted up, you can still see the remains of the engines.

Night Diving

The *Cement Barge* is always worth a visit and is excellent for most types of training dives, as well as offering some of the best night diving around. Only a short journey from most of the harbours on the west coast, this reef of cement and metal acts as a magnet to a great variety of fish, night and day.

Arabian angel-fish

Marine Life

There's always a variety and an abundance of fish on this wreck, which has several resident clownfish nestling within the anemones. The marine growth is well established, with sponges, thorny oysters, sea squirts, clams, scallops and barnacles covering every available surface, including the cement bags. The holes and cracks hide a variety of fish, including hammour (although they tend to be small since this wreck is well fished). Despite being a popular fishing spot, the fish are very tame and will crowd around divers. On one particular dive, we were 'mobbed' by Arabian angel-fish, batfish and sergeant majors!

Gobies and their symbiotic shrimp can be seen in the sand surrounding the hull. The gobies guard the hole while the shrimp busily work clearing sand from their home. However, you'll have to be very patient to see the shrimp since they dart back into the safety of their home at any sign of movement. Look out for blennies in small holes, as well as several species of dottybacks; small, beautifully coloured fish that are always nearby in search of a titbit.

Goby with commensal shrimp

There are also large shoals of yellow snappers surrounding the wreck and sometimes large patrolling schools of juvenile barracuda. Watch out for stingrays since they are usually covered by sand with only the tail visible.

Shrimp hiding in anemone for safety

Snorkelling

This is one of the few wrecks where it is shallow enough to make snorkelling possible. With the cabin at 5 metres and the deck and holds at 8-10 metres, it can easily be seen from the surface. For those with a good lung capacity, the whole of the top section is worth a swim down to explore.

44

Diving the West Coast ⠿ Cement Barge (Alamina)

DB1/SMB

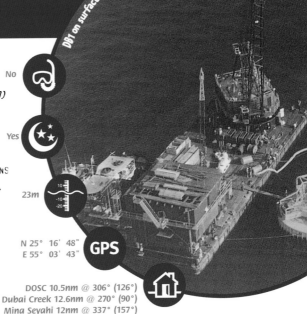

DB1 on surface

WRECK REGISTER 108300067

NAME: *DERRICK BARGE 1 OR DB1 (OR SHEIKH MOHAMMED'S BARGE/SMB)*

NATIONALITY: USA

LAUNCHED: OCTOBER 8, 1962

TYPE: PURPOSE BUILT TOWING DERRICK BARGE

TONNAGE: APPROXIMATELY 2,700 TONS

DIMENSIONS: L: 55M, B: 21M, D: 6M, H: 10M

CARGO: NONE

DATE SUNK: JULY 20, 1984

CHARTED DEPTH: 23 METRES

No

Yes

23m

N 25° 16' 48"
E 55° 03' 43" **GPS**

DOSC 10.5nm @ 306° (126°)
Dubai Creek 12.6nm @ 270° (90°)
Mina Seyahi 12nm @ 337° (157°)

Circumstances of Loss

Sunk by the UAE armed forces to create an artificial reef.

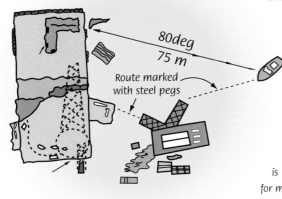

80deg
75 m

Route marked
with steel pegs

Details

The *Derrick Barge (DB1)* is also known as Sheikh Mohammed's Barge (SMB) because His Highness agreed to the upkeep of the marker buoy in perpetuity. Usually a north cardinal buoy is used, but when it is removed for maintenance, it is replaced with an isolated danger buoy.

The *DB1* was a purpose-built towing barge, constructed for McDermott's in Harvey, Louisiana USA, and completed on October 8, 1962. She had three decks, a helicopter pad on the stern and a 1,500 ton American crane on the bow.

The wreck lies upside down in 23 metres of water on a flat, sandy bottom. Having been submerged for more than 16 years, the marine growth on the *DB1* is well-established. She has an overall red-brown colour, from red and black sea squirts, and pearl and thorny oysters. Heavy clamshells, scallops and a variety of sponges grow on their shells, giving the *DB1* its distinctive colour. Carole's first impression in 1989, as recorded in her logbook, describes the wreck as 'like a large cake with lots of frosted icing on it'.

Oyster shell

The crane can still be identified, although most of her superstructure has collapsed into the sand due to the weight of the wreck. The hull has broken in two, making several large holes on the uppermost sections.

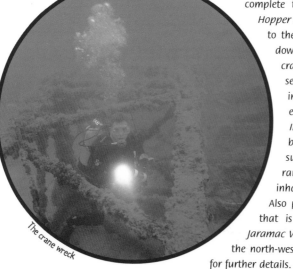

The crane wreck

At the time of sinking, other surplus vessels and wrecks were scuttled around the *DB1* to complete the reef. The largest is the *Hopper Barge*, which is about 35 metres to the east, and is also lying upside down on the boom section of a crane. To the south, there are several pieces of oilfield debris, including a GMC pickup. To the east, 75 metres away, the *Jaramac III* tug sits upright on the seabed, but with a collapsed superstructure. This wreck is rarely visited and is usually inhabited by large shoals of fish. Also part of this site, but a wreck that is dived on its own, is the *Jaramac V*. It lies 200 metres away to the north-west. Refer to the *Jaramac V* for further details.

Diving

The DB1 is one of the most interesting of the wreck dives and the site is so large that groups of divers exploring at the same time often do not see one another. It takes many dives to become familiar with the area and most people only have a clear understanding of what they have been diving on when the visibility reaches 15-20 metres.

There are numerous holes in the wrecks for the more adventurous to investigate. The *DB1's* hull is breaking up, but great care should be taken when exploring inside as parts of it are collapsing and there are many jagged edges. The interior is very silted; take care not to stir it up.

Shoal of barracuda

Suggested Dive Plan A good dive plan would involve heading around the wreck on the seabed, where the greatest depth is covered at the beginning (23 metres), then moving up the sides of the wreck looking for small creatures such as nudibranchs, crabs and shrimps. This way you will end the dive on the upturned hull (16 metres). Don't forget to leave enough air to do a safety stop on the anchor rope.

Stinging hydrocorals

Marine Life

Hydrocorals fill the gaps, making the edges of the wreck indistinct. These corals sting and may leave an irritating rash. It's not unusual to see a sea snake, but beware, don't try to touch them; they are ten times more venomous than land snakes!

Arabian angelfish and wrasse pick over encrustations, and large groups of snappers and

47

fusiliers also make this site home – the shoal opens as you swim through, then closes behind you. Just off the wreck, jacks and barracuda patrol in search of dinner. If you are first down on the site, or at least first on one side, stay high on the hull and swim along the edges looking down on the sand. You may see stingrays feeding on shellfish, and, if you are lucky, a sand shark, Commonly known as guitar sharks, they are not actually sharks, but shovelnose rays that feed on shellfish and crustaceans.

Shoal of snappers

Wreck of 4X4

Energy Determination

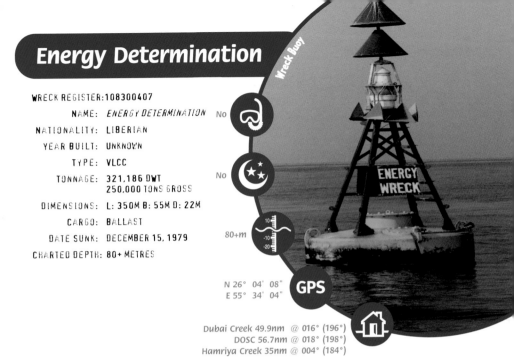

WRECK REGISTER: 108300407
NAME: *ENERGY DETERMINATION*
NATIONALITY: LIBERIAN
YEAR BUILT: UNKNOWN
TYPE: VLCC
TONNAGE: 321,186 DWT
250,000 TONS GROSS
DIMENSIONS: L: 350M B: 55M D: 22M
CARGO: BALLAST
DATE SUNK: DECEMBER 15, 1979
CHARTED DEPTH: 80+ METRES

Wreck Buoy

No

No

80+m

N 26° 04' 08"
E 55° 34' 04"

GPS

Dubai Creek 49.9nm @ 016° (196°)
DOSC 56.7nm @ 018° (198°)
Hamriya Creek 35nm @ 004° (184°)

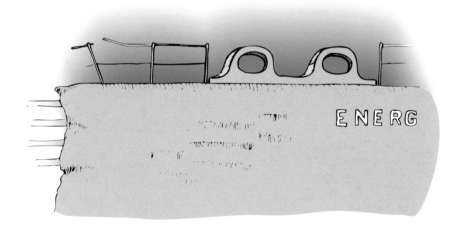

Circumstances of Loss

The *Energy Determination* sailed with ballast from Bonaire, Netherlands Antilles on
November 5, 1979, bound for Das Island in the Gulf, where she was due to load a

cargo of crude oil. At 01:00 local time, December 13, when passing through the Strait of Hormuz, 11 miles off Quoin Island (about 40 miles from Ras Al Khaimah), there was an enormous explosion near the number 9 starboard tank, which contained 354 tons of slops. Fire and smoke raged through the engine room and living quarters. The captain decided to abandon ship and of her crew of 38, 37 were safely picked up from their life rafts by an Omani Naval vessel. One Able Seaman was never found. The survivors were landed at Ras Al Khaimah before being taken to Dubai.

Energy Determination on fire

Meanwhile, the fiercely blazing *Energy Determination*, visible over nine miles away and with burning fuel oil leaking from a hole in her starboard side, began to list and settle by the stern. Salvage tugs, which had raced to the scene, noted that the deck and starboard side had been blown open some 13 metres from the bridge house towards the bow. The salvage crews managed to get a line on board, towing the crippled ship to a safe position clear of the shipping lanes. The fire was now raging below the engine room and a series of explosions blew out all ring tanks on both sides. The superstructure finally collapsed and the deck ripped open.

At 04:30, December 15, *Energy Determination* broke in two, 27 metres forward of the bridge superstructure. The stern section containing the engine room, accommodation and pump room sank east of Mina Saqr at a depth of approximately 80 metres. The bow section was towed towards Dubai and anchored seven miles off the coast for over two years until it was decided to sell it to South

Energy Determination on surface

Korean ship-breakers. She left Dubai under tow on March 1, 1982.

The insurance value of the hull and machinery was US$58 million, making her, up until December 1988, the largest constructive total hull loss ever underwritten by Lloyd's.

Green whip corals

Details

The vessel's stern section rests on her port side in 80-90 metres of water. The wreck is on an incline; the depth from the surface to the top of the wreck is about 25 metres at the forward starboard section, descending to 60 metres at the stern end. The accommodation deck and machinery flat (i.e. the cabin-like structure over the engine room), are more or less intact, but the bridge is canted over and partially torn off. The deck and tank directly forward of the accommodation area have been ripped out, leaving a big jagged hole with ladders running down into the darkness. This gaping hole extends forward for about 10 metres to where the deck and hull remain intact. The remaining 25 metres of deck and hull come to an abrupt end where the bow section broke off.

Diver in wreck on deck

Diving

Diving the *Energy Determination* is not for the inexperienced or faint-hearted. Great care must be taken in the preparation and planning for this dive. The currents can run at over 5 knots, so you should plan to dive in slack water in neap tides. Tide tables are generally only available for Port Rashid and Khor Fakkan, so some calculations must be made to determine slack water. You should plan to be on site early to allow for tidal differences in the locality.

Anchoring onto the wreck can be very time consuming due to the depth and current the line bellies out, not allowing the anchor to reach the wreck. Instead, the preferred method is to use a redundant shot line and not to anchor. For safety, an additional cylinder and regulator should be rigged on the shot line at 10 metres.

Marble ray

Marine Life

The forward 25 metre section of the hull is covered in yellow, white and red soft corals, and some lime green whip corals. Strong currents keep these corals clean and colourful when you swim down, these bright corals glowing in the gloom are the first things you see. The fish are bigger and tamer; you may see large, frightening, but surprisingly tame marble rays, or a whale shark (one has been photographed at close quarters on this wreck).

Whip corals

Hopper Barge 6

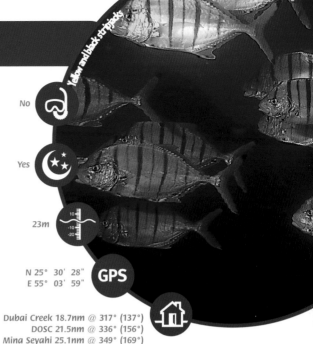

Yellow and black stripjacks

WRECK REGISTER: —

NAME:	*HOPPER BARGE 6 (HB6)*
NATIONALITY:	PANAMANIAN REGISTERED
YEAR BUILT:	UNKNOWN
TYPE:	DUMP BARGE
TONNAGE:	1,000 TONS GROSS
DIMENSIONS:	L: 48M, B: 14M, D: 5M
CARGO:	NONE
DATE SUNK:	ABOUT 1985
CHARTED DEPTH:	23 METRES

No

Yes

23m

N 25° 30' 28"
E 55° 03' 59" **GPS**

Dubai Creek 18.7nm @ 317° (137°)
DOSC 21.5nm @ 336° (156°)
Mina Seyahi 25.1nm @ 349° (169°)
Neptune to Hopper Barge 0.18nm @ 223° (43°)

Circumstances of Loss

Sunk by local fishermen to form an artificial offshore reef.

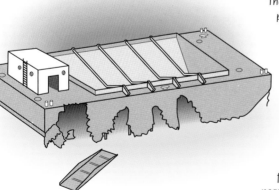

There are several wrecks in close proximity to the Neptune marker buoy. Under International Maritime law, wrecks forming a hazard to shipping must have a marker buoy indicating where there is clear water. These are known as cardinal marker buoys. However, the upkeep and maintenance of these buoys is costly (in excess of US$50,000 a year), so fishermen tend to sink vessels near to existing marker buoys, rather than incur the cost of a new buoy.

Details

During a storm on February 18, 1982, the HB6 drifted onto the lee breakwater of Port Khalid in Sharjah, resulting in a total loss insurance claim. She was later raised, towed to her present location and sunk. Her drop-bottom doors were hydraulically operated, and you can see the two cabins which housed the hydraulic gear on the stern. A large cavity on the starboard side, a result of the collision with the breakwater stabits, is also visible.

Four eyed cowrie

Diving

This is an easy wreck for navigation as she is sitting upright in 25 metres, with her bows facing south at 180°, and situated very close to the Neptune. Her starboard side is beginning to break up and several large holes have exposed the drop-bottom doors. The holes in the side are well worth a visit, best explored with a torch. Entry into the machinery cabins is also possible.

Guitar shark

Marine Life

On a recent visit to the HB6, when exploring one of the larger holes under the wreck, we found several empty Cypraea pulchar cowries. Known locally as 'four-eyes', these beautiful shells are light pinkish brown with two chocolate brown blotches at each extremity.

On ascending at the end of the dive, batfish follow you nearly all the way to the surface. These large fish show no fear of divers and are rarely for sale in the markets, so their friendliness could be explained by the fact that fishermen do not target them.

Jaramac V

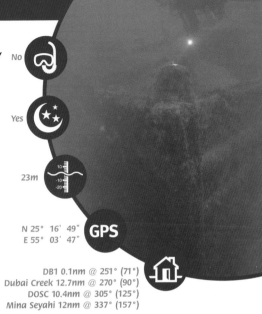

WRECK REGISTER: —
NAME: MCDERMOTT'S JARAMAC V
NATIONALITY: USA
YEAR BUILT: UNKNOWN
TYPE: PURPOSE BUILT TUG
TONNAGE: GROSS 119
NET 80 TONS
DIMENSIONS: L: 24.5M, B: 6.9M,
D: 2.7M
CARGO: NONE
DATE SUNK: JULY 20, 1984
CHARTED DEPTH: 23 METRES

No

Yes

23m

N 25° 16' 49"
E 55° 03' 47" **GPS**

DB1 0.1nm @ 251° (71°)
Dubai Creek 12.7nm @ 270° (90°)
DOSC 10.4nm @ 305° (125°)
Mina Seyahi 12nm @ 337° (157°)

Circumstances of Loss

Sunk by the UAE armed forces to create
an artificial reef.

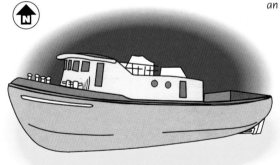

Details

This was a twin-screw utility tug,
with two 12V-71 General Motors
diesel engines producing
1000HP.

For further details of the
sinking, refer to the DB1, West
Coast dives.

Diving

The Jaramac V sits upright on the seabed
and is more or less intact. Exploring the wreck
is very easy and you can access the bridge, engine

55

room and accommodation quarters without too much effort. This small wreck is visited infrequently and is usually home to larger marine life.

If you find the wreck too small you can swim over to the *DB1*, which is lying approximately 200 metres to the south-east. The route between the two sites is marked by a row of pegs placed by the local BSAC Club 1339.

Jellyfish with juveniles

Marine Life

The fish here are not very nervous, so you can get close to observe them. Swim around the lower part of the wreck first, searching on the sandy bottom for stingrays, then close in to see hammour and small snappers darting in and out of the crevices where the hull rests on the sand. Moving up to the superstructure, you'll find black spotted pufferfish; regular residents patrolling the hatches, companionways and cabins at all hours. At night, these fish are temporarily blinded by bright light and go crashing into any obstruction in their path.

Stingray

Once, while making a safety stop on the anchor line a most magnificent jellyfish drifted slowly by. It was nearly transparent, but with a slightly milky white bell-shaped mantle. Darting in and out of the long tentacles was a shoal of tiny juvenile jacks – fascinating!

Jumeirah Artificial Reef

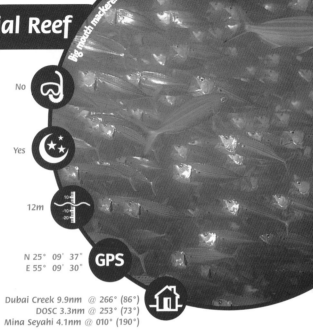

Big mouth mackerel

NAME: JUMEIRAH BEACH HOTEL ARTIFICIAL REEF

YEAR BUILT: JULY 1996

LOCATION: 2.5 KM OFFSHORE, IN FRONT OF THE RESORT

DIVE SITE: FLAT SANDY BOTTOM WITH HOLLOW CONCRETE BLOCKS

CHARTED DEPTH: 12 METRES

No

Yes

12m

N 25° 09' 37"
E 55° 09' 30" **GPS**

Dubai Creek 9.9nm @ 266° (86°)
DOSC 3.3nm @ 253° (73°)
Mina Seyahi 4.1nm @ 010° (190°)

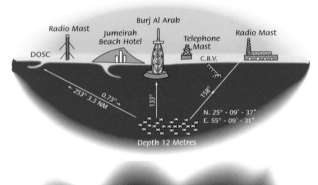

Radio Mast
DOSC
Jumeirah Beach Hotel
Burj Al Arab
Telephone Mast
C.B.V.
Radio Mast

← 253° 3.3 NM
0.73°→
133°
158°

N. 25° - 09' - 37"
E. 55° - 09' - 31"

Depth 12 Metres

Details

During the construction of the Burj Al Arab Hotel, there was a surplus of approximately three thousand hollow concrete foundation blocks (see the base of the island for examples). These one metre square blocks are known as SHEDS (Shepherd Hill Energy Dissipaters), and are statistically proven as one of the finest havens for marine life available to reef engineers.

It was decided to form an artificial reef and marine park with the blocks, and in July 1996 the reef was constructed in 12 metres of water. It is built in a herringbone shape, approximately 100 x 30 metres in size.

The blocks were placed two-high by a small derrick barge. The construction was positioned at an angle, so that each side of the reef offers different attractions for marine life.

Close up of the blocks

Diving

The herringbone design provides plenty of gullies and crevices for the fish. The seaward side is a feeding ground for pelagic species and a great environment for current loving corals to grow. This is also where you are most likely to encounter larger species of fish, such as shark or barracuda. The coastal side of the reef offers protection from the current and is an ideal home for a wealth of marine life, smaller fish and more delicate coral cover that cannot survive the fast and furious conditions on the seaward side.

The depth from the surface to the top of the blocks is 10 metres and 12 metres to the sand. If you want to dive this artificial reef, which belongs to the hotel, you should contact the Pavilion Dive Centre, Jumeirah Beach Hotel.

Shoal of jacks

Marine Life

The marine life is now well established and corals are beginning to form, with sponges, thorny oysters, black sea squirts, clams, scallops and ever present barnacles covering every available surface. The hollows and gaps hide a variety of fish, such as hammour, gobies and dottybacks – these beautiful purple and orange fish are always a pleasure to watch. Often large shoals of yellow snappers swim round the blocks, darting away as you close in. You can also see sizeable schools of young barracuda and the occasional larger fish patrolling the site waiting to pounce. Big mouth mackerel and jacks school and feed here as well. Look out for stingrays (the young ones in particular are often completely covered by sand with only the tail visible), and beware of sea snakes, which seem to come closer to shore in winter.

Barnacles

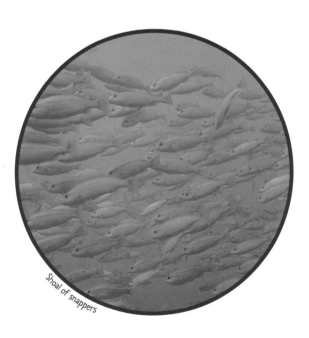

Shoal of snappers

MV Dara

Dara on surface

WRECK REGISTER: 108300171
NAME: *MV DARA*
NATIONALITY: BRITISH
YEAR BUILT: 1948
TYPE: PASSENGER LINER
TONNAGE: 5,030 TONS
DIMENSIONS: L: 121M, B: 17M, D: 15M
CARGO: MAIL AND CARGO
DATE SUNK: APRIL 10, 1961
CHARTED DEPTH: 20 METRES

No

Yes

20m

N 25° 34' 29"
E 55° 27' 58"

GPS

DOSC 27.4nm @ 28° (208°)
Dubai Creek 20.3nm @ 025° (205°)
Hamriya Creek 6.2nm @ 339° (159°)

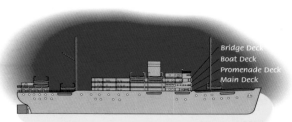

Bridge Deck
Boat Deck
Promenade Deck
Main Deck

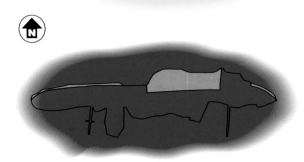

Circumstances of Loss

The MV Dara caught fire following an explosion between decks. Although the fire was eventually extinguished after two days, the ship sank while under tow by the salvage vessel Ocean Salvor.

Details

The MV Dara was a passenger liner fitted with a single Doxford oil engine, built by Barclay Curle & Co., Glasgow, UK and operated by the British India Steam Navigation Company. Nowadays, the MV Dara is officially owned by Clive Frost of Aqua Diving Services.

The story of the disaster is well documented. The following information has been compiled from 'Last Hours on the Dara' by P.J. Abraham, 'The Grey-Widow Maker' by Bernard Edward and an article by Ian Bain in the Khaleej Times Magazine, April 4, 1980.

Telesto corals

The Dara sailed between Bombay, Karachi, the Gulf and the ports of Basra, Kuwait, Bahrain, Dubai and Muscat, carrying passengers, mail and cargo. During the early hours of April 8, 1961, after putting to sea on April 7 to weather out a storm, a bomb planted by an Omani rebel exploded. It is believed that the bomb was timed to explode when the Dara berthed at Muscat, but due to the storm, her departure from Dubai was delayed. The bomb was planted to further the cause of the Dhofar rebellion; the uprising against Sultan Said bin Taimur, the rather erratic and isolated ruler of Oman, who was eventually replaced in a bloodless coup by his son, the present Sultan.

Cockscomb oyster shell

The explosion started a fire that raged for two days and caused considerable loss of life. The final figure was 238 deaths; the greatest number of fatalities recorded at sea in peacetime after the *Titanic* disaster.

Diving

The Dara is lying on her starboard side, broken into three main sections, in 20 metres of water. Every season the superstructure collapses further, limiting access into the wreck, although it is still possible to enter through the stern section. This site can be quite dangerous as the tides can be very strong creating poor visibility. However, on a neap tide this is an excellent dive.

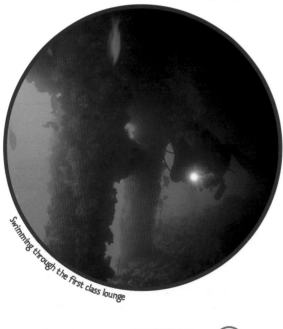

Torpedo ray

Marine Life

One of the unique species of marine life on this site are the cowries; their shells have absorbed the iron oxide from the rusting wreck, giving them a metallic reddy-brown colour. Both the Cypraea histro and Arabica cowries are affected.

The Dara also attracts many species of ray; on one dive, we saw bull stingrays and shovelnose guitarfish feeding on the sand, a feather tailed stingray gliding past and eagle rays overhead.

Swimming through the first class lounge

MV Sarraf Three

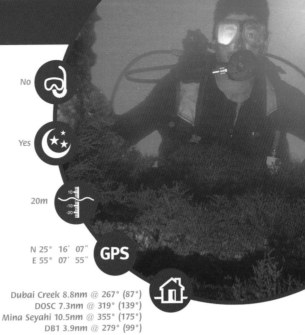

WRECK REGISTER: 108300110

NAME:	*MV SARRAF THREE*
NATIONALITY:	KUWAITI. NO KT 1232
YEAR BUILT:	1935 IN MANNHEIM, GERMANY
TYPE:	COASTAL VESSEL SINGLE SCREW ENGINE
TONNAGE:	288 TONS GROSS
DIMENSIONS:	L: 42M, B: 6.5M, D: 2.6M
CARGO:	NONE
DATE SUNK:	AUGUST 3, 1986
CHARTED DEPTH:	20 METRES

No

Yes

20m

N 25° 16' 07"
E 55° 07' 55" **GPS**

Dubai Creek 8.8nm @ 267° (87°)
DOSC 7.3nm @ 319° (139°)
Mina Seyahi 10.5nm @ 355° (175°)
DB1 3.9nm @ 279° (99°)

Circumstances of Loss

Sunk by a local fisherman to form an artificial offshore reef.

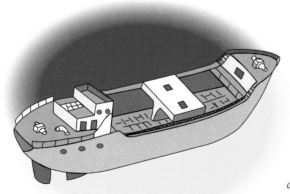

Details

On the night of the 'golf ball' hailstorm on April 30, 1981, while moored at Hamriya Harbour, the *Sarraf* was rammed by the *MV Taiser*. The *Taiser* was being held by the authorities for the non-payment of port dues and was moored off the port side of the *Sarraf Three*. The *Taiser* broke her moorings in the storm, and collided with the smaller vessel, damaging her superstructure and forcing her starboard side onto the inner wall of the main breakwater where she sank on May 3, 1981. *The Sarraf* was raised on June 21, 1981, re-floated and abandoned in Hamriya Port, Dubai.

During the Dubai waterfront clean up in April 1985, interest was shown in the *Sarraf* for the formation of an offshore reef. She was towed to the British Embassy wharf and privately bought in August 1985, then taken out and sunk at her present location. She lies upright and virtually intact (minus her brass fittings), with her bow pointing north. Her last official owners were Hussain Abdulla Al Sarraf & Brothers.

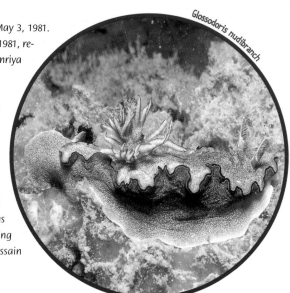

Glossodoris nudibranch

Diving

This site makes a good day or an excellent night dive, with numerous colourful soft corals. It is possible to gain access to the engine room and accommodation deck through the small companionway below the bridge although it can be a tight squeeze. The stern accommodation is filled with silt and great care is needed not to stir it up.

Pufferfish

Marine Life

At night, this wreck is the home of large pufferfish, and small yellow snappers hiding in every nook and cranny, waiting for daylight so that they can congregate around the wreck.

Nasteran

WRECK REGISTER: 108300201
NAME: *NASTERAN*
NATIONALITY: IRANIAN REGISTERED
YEAR BUILT: UNKNOWN
TYPE: LANDING CRAFT
TONNAGE: 652 TONS GROSS
DIMENSIONS: L: 62M, B: 10M, D: 8M
CARGO: STONES
DATE SUNK: MARCH 14, 1970
CHARTED DEPTH: 20 METRES

No

Yes

20m

N 25° 28' 00"
E 55° 21' 22" **GPS**

Dubai Creek 12nm @ 0.15° (195°)
DOSC 18.9nm @ 022° (202°)
Hamriya Creek 7.4nm @ 262° (82°)
Mina Seyahi 25.2nm @ 028° (208°)

Circumstances of Loss
Unknown.

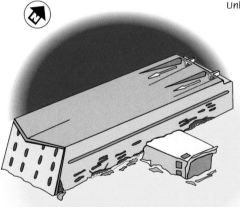

Details
The vessel lies completely upside down in 23 metres of water, with the bow/landing door facing the shore at 150°. The wheelhouse lies to the east, next to the starboard side of the vessel. Both propellers have been cut off.

Diving
Access to the accommodation and engine room is through a hole near the wheelhouse on the east side of the wreck, however, this route is very silted. The deck area

forward of the wheelhouse is also worth a visit, but take a torch/flashlight to illuminate the fish and marine growth. Entry into the cargo area is through the partially open landing doors. If you are lucky, you will find some surprises, such as blind juvenile sharks, hiding in the darker areas of the vessel.

There is a lot of silt throughout the wreck, and care must be taken not to stir up the bottom. If penetrating the Nasteran, it is advisable to use a line and torch at all times.

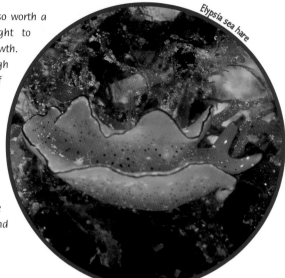
Elypsia sea hare

Marine Life

It is worth exploring the upturned hull for smaller creatures which are often overlooked; look out for shells, shrimps, nudibranchs, small blennies and sea hares. Sea hares are members of the shell family and are called 'hares' because of their rabbit-like appearance. They have two rolled rhinopores (sensory organs on their head) giving them 'rabbits ears', and two flaps, known as parapodia, to aid swimming. They are herbivorous, meaning that they feed on algae and sea grasses – the hull is a regular smorgasbord for them!

Close up of shell's eyes

Neptune 6

WRECK REGISTER: 108300055
NAME: *NEPTUNE 6*
NATIONALITY: PANAMANIAN REGISTERED
YEAR BUILT: UNKNOWN
TYPE: DRILL RIG TENDER BARGE
TONNAGE: 2300 GROSS
DIMENSIONS: L: 79M, B: 15M, D: 8M
CARGO: GENERAL DRILLING EQUIPMENT
DATE SUNK: NOVEMBER 12, 1973
CHARTED DEPTH: 20 METRES

No

Yes

20m

N 25° 30' 20"
E 55° 03' 50" **GPS**

Dubai Creek 18.7nm @ 317° (137°)
DOSC 21.5nm @ 336° (156°)
Mina Seyahi 25nm @ 349° (168°)

Circumstances of Loss

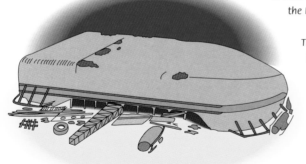

While fighting the world's worst off-shore fire, the *Neptune* was supporting the drilling rig, *WD Kent*, in the Fateh Field as it cross-drilled the burning oil well for the Dubai Petroleum Company.

The *Neptune* pulled off during bad weather, but dragged her anchor and collided with the *WD Kent*, sinking the drill rig. While under tow to Sharjah following the collision, the *Neptune* capsized and sank in her present position.

Details

The vessel lies upside down in 25 metres of water with her bow facing 151°. Along her port side there is a considerable amount of debris, including a crane boom, drilling equipment and wreckage from the deck accommodation.

Diving

There can be strong currents at this site, making exploration quite difficult. For many years, the main entrance into the wreck was on the starboard side, a third of the way along the hull from the stern. However, now that the wreck is breaking up, access is possible on both the port and starboard sides, and you can swim right through. Brass items, mainly lamps from rooms deep inside the wreck, are still being liberated.

Neptune wreck buoy

Although this site is 18.7nm from the shore, it is usually an excellent dive. There are three other wrecks within a 1nm radius of the Neptune; the *Anchor Barge*, *Hopper Barge* and the *Morrafi Barge* (the *Morrafi* is of little interest and rarely dived).

Octocoral

Marine Life

Fish life tends to congregate on the port side, although you can often find stingrays by swimming out beyond the wreckage. The crane structure is home to a colony of white soft coral, which is very beautiful when illuminated.

After looking around the wreck, take the time to look closer at the wreck's surface you will find shrimps, blennies and octocorals (so called because they have eight feather-like tentacles or pinnates.) The

Diving the West Coast Nasteran

octocorals are very small and come in many colours. They can live as individuals or in friendly colonies. Some are purely soft and feathery and some have an internal skeleton composed of a type of calcareous material, while others use another subject as a base to sprout out of. Take the time to watch them feeding; their polyps will pulse and the coral colonies pulsate at various speeds, the effect is quite hypnotic!

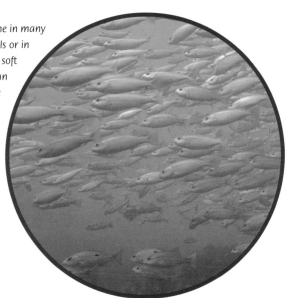

Completing a safety stop

Rashid Wrecks

* MV AFSHAR 2 (FORMERLY ANITCH SCHUTT)
* MV ANT
* LC BEAUTY JUDY
* LC BHATIA
* COLES MOBILE CRANE
* GML 11 LONDON
* MV NASSER
* THREE MISCELLANEOUS FLAT TOP BARGES

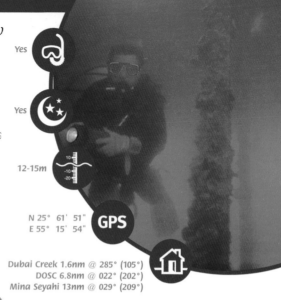

Yes

Yes

12-15m

N 25° 61' 51"
E 55° 15' 54" **GPS**

Dubai Creek 1.6nm @ 285° (105°)
DOSC 6.8nm @ 022° (202°)
Mina Seyahi 13nm @ 029° (209°)

Circumtances of Loss

Along the main breakwater of Dubai Dry Dock is a collection of shipwrecks and other quayside equipment. In 1985, the Dubai Municipality cleaned up the Creek and waterfront and the following vessels were salvaged and re-sunk against the outer dry dock breakwater.

MV Afshar 2

A small freighter of 745 DWT, MV Afshar 2 was built in 1954 in Bremen, Germany and registered in Iran. The forecastle, stern accommodation and wheelhouse of this single screw Baltic coaster are built of aluminium. She is

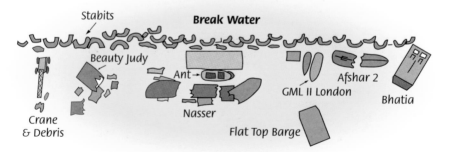

broken into two sections and lies parallel to the breakwater in 15 metres of water. Both sections are upside down; the stern wheelhouse is crushed, but the lower deck is still accessible.

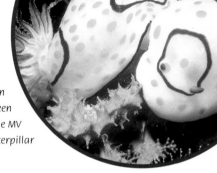

Common nudibranchs

MV Ant

A single screw tug that was built circa 1945 and originally owned by Gray MacKenzie & Co. The *Ant* sits upright in 14 metres of water, sandwiched between a flat top barge and the port side of the MV Nasser. Her wheelhouse and caterpillar engine are still in place.

LC Beauty Judy

This is a 70 metre long converted steel MK 8 landing craft that was built in 1948. She has a gross weight of 1018 tons and was powered by twin Paxman Riccardo diesel engines. Only the stern section remains and is deteriorating badly. The stern is against the breakwater and it is possible to swim through the engine room.

LC Bhatia

The Bhatia is a twin screw landing craft that is lying upside down with her stern nearest the breakwater, giving access to the stern accommodation, wheelhouse, forward chain lockers and bosun's storerooms. This is the furthest south of the wrecks, and is not often visited.

Coles Mobile Crane

This crane marks the northern-most point of the *Rashid* wrecks.

GML 11 London

A single screw tug, built circa 1950, and originally owned by Gray MacKenzie & Co. She lies with her stern against the breakwater in 14 metres of water

Hovering over Rashid wrecks

and is located between the *MV Afshar 2* and the *MV Nasser*.

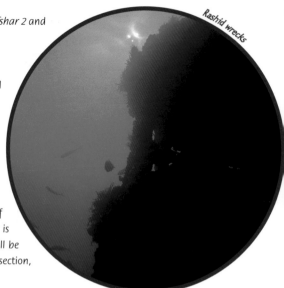
Rashid wrecks

MV Nasser

Built in 1947 by Ardrossan Dockyard Ltd, UK and registered in Abadan, Iran, this is a twin bronze screw cargo vessel. Centre castle DWT 1703. The outermost of three wrecks, the *Nasser* now lies in three sections running parallel to the breakwater. The centre castle section sits upright with the mast rising to within a metre of the surface. The accommodation deck is collapsing (although the toilets can still be seen!). It's very silty inside the main section, so take care not to get disorientated.

Diving

The Rashid wrecks are a wreck diver's dream and a good standby site when the weather is rough, as the harbour wall offers some protection from the heavy seas. Night dives on the wrecks are always great fun, but take care in case you end up in cabins or holds without knowing how to find your way out!

Sea snake

Marine Life

Since this is a relatively shallow site, smaller reef fish abound in all the nooks and crannies.

On one of Tony's many dives here he spotted a sea snake. It appeared to be dead and hung vertically, slowly moving with the wave action, its head lost in a hole in the wreck. After watching this large snake for a while and seeing no sign of life, he moved on, only to find the snake very much alive and following him! Tony swam away furiously, only to find the snake swimming alongside his arm, fascinated by his dive watch! Sea snakes are not aggressive, and we have never heard of any attacks here. However, Tony has never been near one since (and no longer wears shiny chrome watches either!).

Snorkelling

This is another of the West Coast wreck sites where the snorkelling is good. Along the harbour wall, adjacent to the wrecks, a variety of corals and marine life can be seen from the surface. Several wrecks rest on the wall, while others, like the Nasser, have sections of their mast and bridge only a couple of metres below the surface.

Rashid wrecks

Note that this site must be visited by boat. From the shore to the wreck site is over 2 km, making the swim from the shore out along the harbour wall rather impractical.

Anemone shrimp

Zainab

Zainab bridge

WRECK REGISTER: NOT CHARTED

NAME: ZAINAB ORIGINALLY KNOWN AS THE SEASROUN FIVE

NATIONALITY: GEORGIAN REGISTERED

YEAR BUILT: UNKNOWN

TYPE: GENERAL CARGO SHIP

TONNAGE: 1,400 GROSS

DIMENSIONS: L: 70M, B: 12M, D: 5M

CARGO: FUEL OIL

DATE SUNK: APRIL 14, 2001

CHARTED DEPTH: 26 METRES

No

Yes

30m

N 25° 14' 93"
E 54° 51' 54" **GPS**

From Dubai Creek 23.8 nm @ 265° (85°)
From Mina Seyahi 18.1 nm @ 300° (120°)
From DOSC 20 nm @ 281° (101°)

Circumstances of Loss

The Zainab was sunk deliberately by her 11-man crew, to avoid being boarded by the US Navy who were enforcing the UN sanctions on Iraq.

Details

The Zainab, formerly called the Seasroun Five is a general cargo ship with two holds forward and the machinery, bridge and quarters aft.

She sailed under a Georgian flag and was involved in the illegal transportation of light fuel oil from Iraq. Her two holds had been converted to hold the oil in an effort to conceal her illegal cargo. The vessel was carrying approximately 1,300 tonnes of fuel oil.

The sinking caused a major oil spill, coming ashore on the northern gulf coast, causing serious concern to the local gas processing plant as she sank within a few hundred metres of their offshore gas pipelines.

The story of the sinking was documented on several occasions during April 2001 in the Gulf News.

The fire extinguisher at the stern

Diving

The Zainab is intact and lying on her port side, the anchor still sitting snug on the bow. The covers of the holds are off and lying on the sea bed at 30m. There are various bits and pieces strewn over the seabed; an empty compass binnacle, a life raft upside down at the stern and on the seabed below the propeller there is an industrial fire extinguisher.

For those who wish to explore inside the wreck, the bridge, accomodation and engine room are easily accessible. Be sure that you can see daylight at the other end, before you enter the wreck.

The Zainab propeller

Suggested Dive Plan

This is one of the deeper dive sites on this coast and is a fairly large wreck, over 70ms long. You should be able to explore it in one dive. The most interesting area is the deck, now vertical.

Go along the wreck and past the open hatches; their doors haphazardly lying around look like a discarded pack of cards on the seabed. Investigate the upturned life raft when you reach the stern and if you have

enough bottom time glance at the fire
extinguisher sitting just under the
propeller. Ascend slowly, exploring the
bridge and decks aft. The remaining
life raft is swinging from one davit.
Go around the wreck and look at
the propeller. Then return to the
top of the wreck, at approximately
20 meters depth.

Precariously hanging liferaft

Marine Life

During the relatively short time the
Zainab has been down, it has attracted
a large variety of marine life. The wreck
is totally carpeted with small oysters and
juvenile fish weaving in and out of their shell
homes avoiding contact with divers, but some are
very inquisitive and allow you to get very close to them.

You may find large rays resting on the seabed, huge shoals of barracuda circling the
wreck and usually towards the bow you will see large shoals of yellow snappers
swimming round and round the various masts. There
is usually a small shoal of batfish near the
bridge and wheel house area.

Diver swimming through the campanion way

Night Dive

Possible for the more experienced,
but a long way offshore.

West Coast Diver Enjoying Wrecks

Musandam Dives

Musandam Overview Map

Arabian Gulf
Ras Al Khaimah
Dubai
Fujairah
Hatta
Abu Dhabi
UAE
Al Ain
Gulf of Oman
OMAN

Great Quoin Island
Fanaku Island
Ennerdale Rock
Bu Rashid
Kachalu Island
Ruqq Suwayk
Ras Musandam
Jazirat Al Khayl
Jazirat Musandam East Head
Khasab
Jazirat Sawda
Ras Qabr Al Hindi
Jazirat Hamra
White Rock Ras Khaysah
Ras Khaysay
Hard Rock Café Ras Bashin
Jazirat Umm Al Fayyarin
Ras Dillah Ghubbat Ash Shabus Bay
Ras Dillah
Ras Sarkan
Octopus Rock
Ras Marovi
Pearl Island
Ras Lima
Ras Hamra
Lima Rock
Ras Al Khaimah
Caves, The
Bayah Port Dibba

● Harbours
○ Dive sites (Covered)
● Dive sites (not covered)

Diving the Musandam

The Musandam has one of the most rugged, isolated and beautiful coastlines in the world; the towering Hajar Mountains rise directly out of the sea creating spectacular fjord-like scenery. There are endless possibilities for divers, and the sheltered bays also offer a safe environment for snorkellers and non-divers to explore.

The dive sites we have included in the book for this area are aimed at the more adventurous and experienced diver. Sites like Lima Rock and Octopus Rock are some of the best locations that we have dived. Visibility is usually good, up to about 20 metres. The dives are all on the eastern coast and easily accessible from the UAE by dhow or motorboat, without the need to officially enter Oman. However, these sites represent only a very small portion of what is available in the Musandam area. The Peninsular has a huge section of coastline, from Ras Al Khaimah in the very north of the UAE, around Ras Musandam in the Strait of Hormuz, then down the east coast to Dibba, a small fishing village that is partly Emirati and partly Omani.

Khor Habylayn

For divers there are two main ways of exploring this area; either by boat up the East Coast from Dibba or by driving to Khasab, capital of the Musandam. It's always advisable to take your diving qualifications and some form of identification with you.

Dibba By far the easiest way to dive the Musandam is to hire one of the dive boats or dhows operating from the East Coast (most start from Dibba Bayah harbour). You do not require an Omani visa for this route, even though you technically enter Omani territory, however, you are not allowed

to land. The boats operating in the area are
Omani registered.

Trips can be booked through the dive
centres, and, unless your operator has
agreed to supply them, you will need
to take all your own diving gear,
including tanks.

To reach Dibba Bayah, which is in the
Omani part of Dibba, you will need to
first go through the UAE part of the
town. No visa is required.

Khasab The other option for exploring the
Musandam is to go overland to Khasab, via
the west coast road through Ras Al Khaimah,
and to contact one of the diving centres there. You
can take your own diving equipment with you, but dive tanks
are sometimes refused entry, since the Omanis want to restrict diving to registered
dive organisations.

Pink teddy bear corals

To enter the Musandam Peninsular you will need a
visa. Visa requirements vary depending on
your nationality and according to whether
you are a UAE resident or a visitor.
Remember that regulations in this part
of the world often change virtually
overnight, so check details before
you leave to avoid disappointment.

There are UAE and Omani border
posts at the entrance point to the
Musandam, so the correct UAE
visa is required for visitors to
return to the Emirates.

If you have been a UAE resident for
at least a year and fulfil certain
criteria, a visa can be obtained on
arrival at the border, otherwise apply at the
Omani Embassy in Abu Dhabi (02 446 3333)

Octocorals

or the Consulate in Dubai (04 397 1000). The fee is Dhs.70 (Dhs.200 if you are British!). Visas usually take about four days to process, although sometimes they are able to speed things up for you.

British and American citizens with UAE residency who are planning many visits to Oman may consider applying for a two year multiple entry visa. This costs Dhs.400.

The local currency is the Omani Riyal (referred to as RO or OR), which is divided into 1,000 baisa (or baiza). The exchange rate is usually about Dhs.10 = RO.1. However, dirhams are widely accepted.

Rock formations in Musandam

Note that, by car, UAE expats can only enter and exit the Musandam on the Ras Al Khaimah side of the peninsula, not through Wadi Bih.

Night Diving

We have dived most of the sites mentioned in this area at night with great success. Less experienced divers will probably find the currents a greater problem at night than in the daytime.

Juvenile octopus in shell

You will have to plan the trip with your dive operator well in advance and expect to pay extra. Operators are generally less keen to arrange a night dive, unless you book an overnight trip or one lasting several days. In addition, unloading a boat full of dive gear late at night in Dibba Bayah harbour with its high harbour walls can create its own difficulties! The live aboard boat, The Charlotte Anne, offers night diving in their packages.

Diver Safety

Remember the following points so that your Musandam dives are safe and pleasant.

• Follow the dive plan given by the operator, especially if it is your first time on the site and you do not have a dive guide with you.

• Be aware that the currents, upward and downward, can be challenging for even the most experienced of divers. Dive operators usually run drift dives.

• It is recommended that you use an SMB (surface marker buoy). Many divers have a lot of fun with these, attempting to outdo all others with the most original SMB. Instead of buying an SMB from a dive shop, you can purchase all sorts of plastic toys and adapt them, but take care that yours doesn't fly away!

Diver with SMB

Operators

There are a handful of operators specialising in diving the Musandam. Of note are Leema Coast Sea Travels & Diving, with Captain Ali Mohammed, and The Charlotte Anne, which offers 3-7 day live aboard trips. Refer to the Dive Directory for contact details.

If you have your own vessel and wish to travel to the Musandam, you must seek special permission from the Omani Coastguard at Dibba Bayah harbour coastguard post.

Lima Rock

The Caves

The cave entrance

OTHER NAMES: KHOR MALA CAVES

DIVE TYPE: FLAT AND SANDY BOTTOM WITH LIMESTONE CAVERNS

Yes

Dibba Bayah Harbour 10.6nm @ 028° (208°)

Details

These caves are not visible from the surface, but are located about 500 metres away from the pointed rock stack. Erosion by the sea has cut these caves deep into the limestone rock face. The main chamber is an undercut section running into the rock for about 15-20 metres. The bottom is sandy with boulders at about 10 metres. There are several deeper caves at the back of the main chamber.

Yes

N 25° 48' 14"
E 56° 22' 03"

GPS

10m

Diving

This is a good third dive of the day as it is shallow and doesn't go too deep into the rock face, making it ideal for those with a 100 or so bar of air left in their cylinders. A bright torch/flashlight is essential. This is a good site for peeking into holes and tunnels, and for general exploring.

The Musandam Coast

500 Metres

← To Dibba   To Lima →

Night Diving

It is also an excellent site for a night dive as the rock offers some protection from the elements. Look out for all types of crustaceans and marine life coming out to feed.

Marine Life

Enter the caves slowly, looking on the sandy bottom for stingrays and resting reef sharks. As you move into the caves, there will be large shoals of golden cardinal fish in curtains of red and silver guarding the deeper crevices. These caves attract many varieties of small fish seeking the safety and food that these nooks and crannies offer.

Cleaner shrimps hide in the hollows – the white and brown variety can usually be spotted by their tentacles sticking out of their hiding places. If you are fortunate, you may spot some spiny lobsters hiding deep in the cracks.

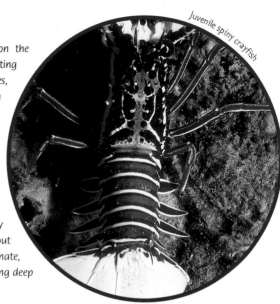

Juvenile spiny crayfish

Snorkelling

Snorkelling can be very good. Swim along the rock wall and duck dive into the entrance of the cave – the roof is just above the surface. Again, a good torch/flashlight is necessary to make the most of this location.

Nudibranch in purple corals

Lima Rock

OTHER NAMES: JAZIRAT LIMA NORTH AND
SOUTH SIDES

DIVE TYPE: BOULDERS, FALLEN ROCK AND
REEF DROPPING DOWN TO
A SANDY BOTTOM WITH
LIMESTONE CAVERNS

Yes

Dibba Bayah Harbour 20.3nm @ 029° (209°)

Details

Another great dive! Lying due north of Dibba, Lima Rock marks the southern entrance to Lima Bay amidst a plethora of coral and marine life. This small island is a pinnacle of limestone rock approximately 800 metres long by 200 metres wide with steep, jagged sides. The waves have undercut the rock in many places, leaving shallow caves and deep fissures. Sheer cliffs drop almost vertically into the water to a depth of around 12 metres, then boulders and scree run steeply down to a sandy bottom at more than 60 metres.

Yes

N 25° 56' 27"
E 56° 27' 51"   **GPS**

12-60m

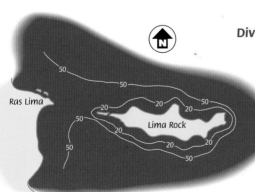

Ras Lima

Lima Rock

Diving

The beauty of Lima Rock is that it can be dived in most weather and tidal conditions. If the sea is rough, or the current is running on one side, the other flank is usually calm. Beware of the currents at the eastern and western tips of the island.

On the southern side of the island, there are a couple of relatively deep caves, one of which used to be the home of a 2.5 metre nurse shark, now only seen very occasionally. At the south-eastern end of the island, a massive boulder guards the easternmost tip of the island. If the currents are mild, wait on this monolith and look out into the deep water for tuna, jacks, sharks and manta rays.

Between 12-20 metres, the boulder field is covered with hard corals (table, staghorn, brain and boulder coral), and patches of soft corals (orange and pink teddy bear coral). The marine life is abundant, with large shoals of reef fish.

Eagle ray

At 20 metres and deeper, abundant yellow and green coloured black coral, and numerous clumps of purple coral appear between the patches of sand, creating a very beautiful site. Look out for yellow-mouthed morays that look as if they have just returned from the paint shop with their vivid, colourful markings! Moving deeper towards the shelving sand, white tip sharks and leopard sharks are often spotted resting on the bottom.

Triggerfish

On the north side, steep walls drop down to the sand at 20 metres. This side of the island is in shade from mid morning onwards.

The island is also home to a variety of birds; ospreys, swifts and sooty falcons frequent the high ramparts of the rock, making it an interesting location to wait between dives.

Snorkelling

The north side of the island offers more shelter if you keep close to the rock face.

Octopus Rock

OTHER NAMES: THE STACK

DIVE TYPE: BOULDERS, FALLEN ROCK AND CORAL REEF, SLOPING TO A SANDY BOTTOM

Yes

Lionfish

Dibba Bayah Harbour 23nm @ 022° (202°)

Yes

Details

With its distinctive undercut top, this isolated stack lies 3 km offshore to the north of Lima and is another great Musandam dive site. The almost round rock is approximately 50 metres in diameter and its sides drop more or less vertically to a mixed rock and sand seabed.

N 26° 00' 02"
E 56° 26' 20"

GPS

5-20m

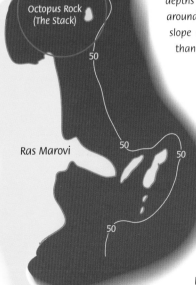

Octopus Rock
(The Stack)

50

Ras Marovi

50

50

50

N

The rocky bottom runs in ridges to the west and north, forming sandy-bottomed gullies. The depths of the gullies vary from 15-20 metres around the base of the rock, then to the south-east slope off onto a sandy seabed descending more than 50 metres.

Diving

Octopus Rock is a marine zoo that can be enjoyed in most weather and tidal conditions due to its sheltered location in Lima Bay. After reaching the bottom, swim north from the base of the rock and you will reach a rocky cliff, running east to west. This leads to the gullies, which are a continuation of the cliff. Most divers turn back at the cliff and circle around the terraces of rock that surround the stack. If you continue, remember to take note of your bearings, since you can end up a long way from the rock.

Marine Life

The stack is a gathering point for an enormous variety of shoaling fish life. Close to the rock you will find numerous reef fish, while further out are jacks, trevally, tuna, barracuda, rays and sharks (if you are lucky). Soft and hard corals abound; green coloured black coral and purple soft coral whips predominate, mixed with the pink and orange of teddybear corals, to create a kaleidoscope of colour.

Jacks

The rocks are home to fanworms, featherstars, juvenile crayfish and anemones. Look under overhangs and in hollows for black or red lionfish, but take care as these fish are poisonous. On most dives, stingrays can be seen feeding in the sand or resting under boulder coral overhangs. You also have a good chance of seeing nurse and leopard sharks.

Yellow sweetlips

Snorkelling

Snorkelling is very good, especially around the stack. To make the most of this site you will have to duck dive down the sides of the stack. Alternatively, swim away from the stack to the north-west. There are large outcrops of rock 5-8 metres from the surface that are always alive with reef fish.

Pearl Island

Clownfish in anemone

OTHER NAMES: OAKLEY ISLAND

DIVE TYPE: REEF AND SANDY BOTTOM   Yes

Dibba Bayah Harbour 20.6nm @ 031° (211°)

Details

Located in Lima Bay, Pearl Island lies
close to shore, just north of Lima. The
water off the east tip of this rocky island is
about 12 metres deep, gradually becoming
shallower at the sand bar on the west side.
The coral reef surrounding most of the island,
descends gently from a depth of 5 metres to a
sandy bottom.

Yes

N 25° 57' 37"
E 56° 25' 52"   **GPS**

5-12m

Diving

Since it takes approximately 50-60 minutes to swim around the island and because of
the depth, it makes a good second dive with plenty to see.

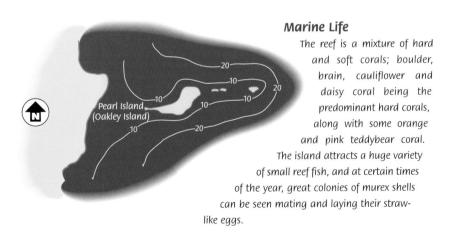

Pearl Island
(Oakley Island)

Marine Life

The reef is a mixture of hard
and soft corals; boulder,
brain, cauliflower and
daisy coral being the
predominant hard corals,
along with some orange
and pink teddybear coral.
The island attracts a huge variety
of small reef fish, and at certain times
of the year, great colonies of murex shells
can be seen mating and laying their straw-
like eggs.

The first thing you hear are parrotfish crunching the coral. Then as you approach these pink, blue and green pastel coloured fish, they swim off leaving a trail of coral particles. There are several patches of anemones dotted around the island, attended by their resident clownfish. If you are wearing brightly coloured gloves, especially yellow, and wave them near these little clowns they will try and attack! The assaults are harmless (although for a small fish, they deliver a nasty bite!), and the fish soon tire of the fun and return to the safety of their poisonous hosts.

Murex shell laying Eggs

Snorkelling

For snorkellers, this island is a pearl(!). Corals run most of the way around the island and two rocks break the surface nearby, and there is always a great variety of reef marine life. In addition, the waters are usually very calm, making this a superb snorkelling site.

Orange hermit crab in shell

Ras Hamra

OTHER NAMES: —

DIVE TYPE: FALLEN ROCK AND CORAL REEF DROPPING TO A SANDY BOTTOM   Yes

Dibba Bayah Harbour 18.8nm @ 028° (208°)

Yes

teddybear corals

Details

The dive site starts at the point at Ras Hamra and runs west along the north cliff face. It is a north-facing site and is in shade by the early afternoon – to see this colourful coral wonderland, you need to dive early in the morning when the sun illuminates the depths. There are several large boulders breaking the surface near the headland.

N 25° 55' 21"
E 56° 26' 39"   **GPS**

5-16m

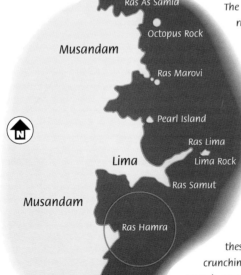

The boulder coral on this site is extensive, running along the side of the cliff from 5 metres down to 16 metres, where the coral reef gently runs down to the sandy bottom. Every available gap is filled with a variety of corals, from brain, daisy and tables of staghorn to great clumps of cauliflower coral fighting for space between the boulder coral.

Diving

This is a shallow site with the corals covering most of the fallen rocks down to a depth of 16 metres. When diving in these areas of hard coral, the sound of crunching fills your ears as the parrotfish munch away at the coral.

Marine Life

This is a good site for reef fish as there are lots of hollows and gaps where the fish dart in and out, playing 'hide and seek'. You will also often see turtles resting between the clumps of coral.

Look into dark holes for red striped squirrelfish, waiting in shoals under the overhangs and in dark corners of the coral. These little, big-eyed fish like to stay in the safety of the shadows. Deeper in the gloom are several species of grouper; some brown with blue spots, others red with blue spots. Gliding over the tops of the corals are the real dandies of the reef; emperor angelfish, butterflyfish and bannerfish. Boxfish propel themselves from one gap in the coral to the next, moving like miniature hovercraft. Then there are the solitary beauties like the Picasso triggerfish. You will also find crown of thorns starfish grazing on the coral – when these voracious predators move on, they leave behind the bleached white skeletons of their former hosts.

Clownfish

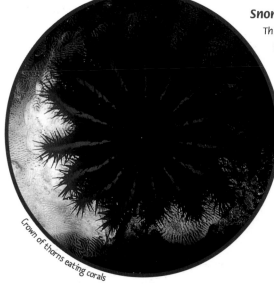

Crown of thorns eating corals

Snorkelling

This is an excellent site for snorkellers, as the reef starts at 5 metres, and you can see as much, if not more, than divers. Duck dive down and explore under the corals, or just drift over the reef without leaving the surface and admire the marine zoo.

Ras Lima

OTHER NAMES: —

DIVE TYPE: BOULDERS, FALLEN
ROCK AND SLOPING REEF
TO A SANDY BOTTOM

Yes

Dibba Bayah Harbour 20.4nm @ 028° (208°)

Yes

N 25° 56' 46"
E 56° 27' 31"

GPS

6-20m

Details

The Ras Lima headland has two dive sites; the north-facing site in Lima Bay and the east bay just south of the headland. The north site is an interesting wall dive, with a steep cliff face that drops down to 10-15 metres and a tangle of fallen boulders. The east bay is located under the east headland cliffs. These are nearly vertical and plunge into the water to a depth of 6-8 metres where the coral reef gently runs down to the sand at 15 metres plus. Scattered throughout both sites are many large rocks, some forming shallow caves.

Ras As Samid

Octopus Rock

Musandam

Ras Marovi

Pearl Island

Lima

Ras Lima

Lima Rock

Ras Samut

Musandam

Ras Hamra

Diving

The sites are in shadow in the afternoon, so plan to dive early. Both locations can be done in one trip, however, it may be better to investigate each area separately. The headland divides the two sites, so if the tide and currents are running on one side, the other should be calm.

Whichever dive you do first, go down to the edge of the corals and the sand, then work around the bay to the headland. When the currents are mild, swim to the point of the headland and watch the shoals of larger ocean fish waiting to pounce on the reef fish. Close to the shore on the east bay, are some large boulder coral heads with undercuts and plenty of hollows.

Table corals

Marine Life

This is a good site for smaller reef fish and big pelagic fish. Manta rays have been seen here on several occasions, and the area is probably a 'cleaning station' for them.

From 5-15 metres, corals cover most of the boulders that have fallen from the cliffs above. The boulder corals are large, with lots of cavities that make a perfect hideaway for fish like the blue triggerfish. Triggerfish don't seem to mind leaving parts of themselves exposed when they are hiding and you can often see bits of bright blue protruding from their hideaways when swimming overhead!

Stag and table coral fill the gaps between the boulder coral, but diving deeper, teddy bear and purple coral start to take over. At 12-15 metres, yellow coloured black coral gradually gives way to the shelving sandy seabed.

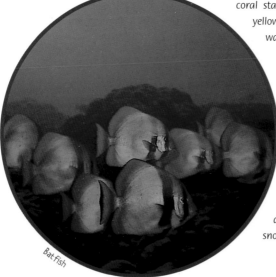

Batfish

Snorkelling

The east bay is an excellent site for snorkellers, with coral starting at 5 metres and some large boulders breaking the surface close to the shoreline. These boulders offer a variety of terrain in easy reach of all levels of ability. The north side of Ras Lima should only be attempted by more experienced snorkellers.

Ras Marovi

OTHER NAMES: —

DIVE TYPE: FALLEN ROCK AND CORAL
REEF DROPPING TO A
SANDY BOTTOM   Yes

Dibba Bayah Harbour 21nm @ 024° (204°)

Yes

N 25° 59' 06"
E 56° 26' 09" **GPS**

6-30m+

White tipped reef shark

Details

Ras Marovi is a collection of four islands; the two larger
islands run in a line south-east from the mainland of Jebel
Al Khatamah. The first large island is separated from the mainland
by a 100 metre channel and the second large island
has a 200 metre channel dividing it from the
first island. The two smaller islands run
south from the most seaward island.
The cliffs of the two larger islands
drop down vertically into the water.
On the north face of the inner
island, the wall is sheer all the way
down to 30 metres.

Diving

The best diving is in the two
channels. The depth of the
channel nearest the shore varies
from 30 metres to the north, rising up
to 6 metres, and then dropping off to 28
metres in the south. The shallowest point of the
second channel is 18 metres, dropping off to over
30 metres on either side. The rocks and boulders

Jebel Ali
Khatamah

Ras
Marovi

slope down to a sandy bottom with a covering of both hard and soft corals. When the currents are running, drift dives through the channels can be great fun.

Rocky channel

Marine Life

There are lots of soft corals on these sites, including plenty of orange and blue teddy bear coral. Purple and yellow coloured black corals are also prevalent.

The islands attract a lot of reef and pelagic fish. In the rock walls there are several shallow caves where large hammour lie in wait for their prey. Leopard sharks, grey reef sharks, white tipped reef sharks and dolphins are regular visitors, while deeper down, stingrays haunt the sandy bottom. In recent years, there have been several sightings of manta rays around the outer island.

Dolphin

Snorkelling

Swim round the edges of the islands. At the deeper points you may see sharks gliding beneath you. The two smaller islands are great for seeing large shoals of fish, but don't forget to duck dive down and explore.

Musandam North of Lima

Since first publishing the **UAE Underwater Explorer**, it has become easier to travel and dive the spectacular northern tip of the Musandam, even the sites in the Strait of Hormuz. Several dive organisations and tour companies now operating in this area offer magical trips. We have received numerous requests to include more dive sites in the second edition. The area is so vast with so many wonderful dives and memorable scenery, it would take another book just to cover the Musandam Peninsula.

We have put together a brief description, including the GPS coordinates, of our favourite, more popular dive sites.

Over the years, the best sites have proved to be around the islands, headlands and promontories. These rocky outcrops in the main current flow attract big sharks, giant trevally, jacks, rays, shoals of tuna, dolphins and the occasional whale shark. The strong currents washing over the corals keep them bright, colourful and healthy. The bays and inlets like Khor Habalayn, though calmer in rough weather, usually have slightly poorer visibility and there is less chance of seeing the bigger species.

As mentioned earlier in the book, diving and exploring this area is very special.

The currents can be very strong so try planning your trips to include sites where you can shelter from the current.

Black Tip Shark

Ras Sarkan

OTHER NAME: UNKNOWN

DIVE TYPE: ROCK WALLS, FALLEN BOULDERS AND CORAL

DEPTH: 6M TO 40M+

GPS: N 26° 04' 36"
E 56° 28' 55"

This dive site is around the headland on the south entrance to Khor Habalayn. The direction of the current will decide which side is dived; both are good. The site consists of fallen rock and coral with patches of sand below 20 metres. Try to make your way to the point of the headland and watch the trevally and tuna feeding in the main current stream.

Ras Dillah

OTHER NAME:	UNKNOWN
DIVE TYPE:	ROCK WALLS, FALLEN BOULDERS AND CORAL
DEPTH:	6M TO 40M+
GPS:	N 26° 07' 51" E 56° 29' 16"

This dive site runs 500 metres into the bay from the north headland tip at the entrance to Khor Habalayn. The shear rock wall drops 15 to 20 metres to the sand and fallen boulders. The rock walls and boulders are covered in black coral. The big pelagic fish tend to gather around the headland. Note this site is in shadow late in the afternoon.

Jacks on patrol

Ras Dillah Ghubbat Ash Shabus Bay

OTHER NAME:	LIGHTHOUSE ROCK
DIVE TYPE:	CORAL REEFS AND BOULDERS
DEPTH:	6M TO 30M+
GPS:	N 26° 08' 37" E 56° 28' 47"

A tall peak resembling a lighthouse dominates this cliff walled bay. Ospreys perch high above the water surveying the dive boats with disdain. The rocks and boulders tumble down into the sea and onto steeply shelving sand. The patches of sand start at about 20 metres and there are huge boulders. You may see feeding stingrays filtering the sand, causing sand storms and leaving slight depressions on the seabed. Undercutting of the rock walls and large boulders have made

Lighthouse rock

overhangs and small caves. Yellow and purple coral cling to all the rocks and boulders. A very colourful dive site, with lots of large fish.

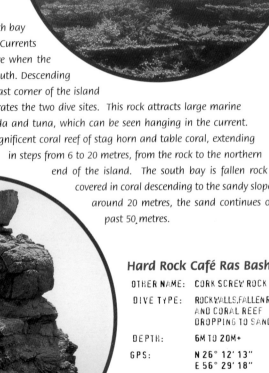

Diver with plate table corals

Jazirat Umm Al Fayyarin

OTHER NAME:	MOTHER OF MOUSE
DIVE TYPE:	ROCK WALLS, FALLEN ROCK AND CORAL REEF SLOPING TO SAND
DEPTH:	6M TO 50M+
GPS:	N 26°10'32" E 56° 32' 47"

The best areas to dive are the south bay and the east side of the island. Currents can be a problem. Plan to dive when the currents are mild or running south. Descending to 50 metres from the south east corner of the island is a rocky outcrop that separates the two dive sites. This rock attracts large marine hunters like jacks, barracuda and tuna, which can be seen hanging in the current. The east side dive is a magnificent coral reef of stag horn and table coral, extending in steps from 6 to 20 metres, from the rock to the northern end of the island. The south bay is fallen rock covered in coral descending to the sandy slope around 20 metres, the sand continues on past 50 metres.

Hard Rock Cafe

Hard Rock Café Ras Bashin

OTHER NAME:	CORK SCREW ROCK
DIVE TYPE:	ROCK WALLS, FALLEN ROCK AND CORAL REEF DROPPING TO SAND
DEPTH:	6M TO 20M+
GPS:	N 26° 12' 13" E 56° 29' 18"

This amazing slender rock pinnacle rises out of the water 8 to 10 metres and looks as if it has been twisted with a rectangular block perched on the top. This is a shallow site of large coral covered boulders and patches of sand. You will see huge shoals of reef fish, the variety and quantity are always surprising. This very colourful site is good for snorkelling.

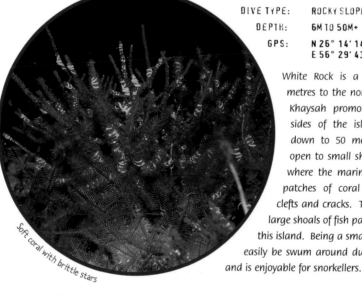

Batfish at a 'cleaning station'

Ras Khaysay

OTHER NAME:	UNKNOWN
DIVE TYPE:	ROCK WALLS, FALLEN ROCK AND CORAL
DEPTH:	6M TO 25M+
GPS:	N 26° 14' 00" E 56° 29' 24"

This narrow rock promontory juts out into the sea for more than a kilometer and lies diagonally across the north and south running currents. This site offers diving in most sea conditions, so if the current is strong on one side it will be sheltered on the other. The cliff walls drop to fallen boulders and coral to about 25 metres.

White Rock, Ras Khaysah

OTHER NAME:	SYDNEY OPERA HOUSE
DIVE TYPE:	ROCKY SLOPES AND CORAL
DEPTH:	6M TO 50M+
GPS:	N 26° 14' 14" E 56° 29' 43"

White Rock is a small island 500 metres to the north east of the Ras Khaysah promontory. The rocky sides of the island drop steeply down to 50 metres+. The sides open to small shelves and fissures where the marine life clings and patches of coral nestle in these clefts and cracks. There are always large shoals of fish patrolling around this island. Being a small island it can easily be swum around during the dive and is enjoyable for snorkellers.

Soft coral with brittle stars

Jazirat Hamra

OTHER NAME:	RED ISLAND
DIVE TYPE:	CORAL REEFS AND BOULDERS
DEPTH:	6M TO 30M+
GPS:	N 26° 16' 54" E 56° 27' 12"

Jazirat Sawda

OTHER NAME:	BLACK ISLAND
DIVE TYPE:	CORAL REEFS AND BOULDERS
DEPTH:	6M TO 30M+
GPS:	N 26° 17' 43" E 56° 27' 12"

Anthias in staghorn coral

Jazirat Sawda and Jazirat Hamra are two islands inside the sheltered bay of Dawhat Ash Shisah. These two islands have a shallow shelving coral reef, which surrounds both islands. The east side is usually dived. The reef runs out into sand at 20 metres. These sites are teeming with reef fish darting in and out of the coral.

Ras Qabr Al Hindi

OTHER NAME:	TIP OF THE INDIAN GRAVE
DIVE TYPE:	CORAL REEFS AND BOULDERS
DEPTH:	6M TO 30M+
GPS:	N 26° 18' 34" E 56° 30' 52"

Whitetip shark

This site extends from the easterly point to the south. At the point the rocky bottom gently slopes to sand at 30 metres. This area is a carpet of velvety coral, occasional rocks and boulders. Further south, the coral is not as abundant and the slope down to the sand is more gradual, with patches of sand starting at 10 to 15 metres. Rays and white tip reef sharks are often seen here.

Jazirat Musandam East Head

OTHER NAME:	PICNIC BAY
DIVE TYPE:	ROCK WALLS, FALLEN ROCK AND CORAL
DEPTH:	6M TO 50M+
GPS:	N 26°22' 11" E 56° 32' 18"

When the currents are strong the sea is a little rough. This headland and bay offer calm water and superb diving. At the point of the headland to the east, the cliff wall drops straight down to 50 metres. Following this wall into the northern bay, it gradually turns into a gentle coral garden slope, where a frenzy of reef fish feed. Sharks and schools of eagle rays may be seen rounding the headland. The gentle coral slopes are very pretty.

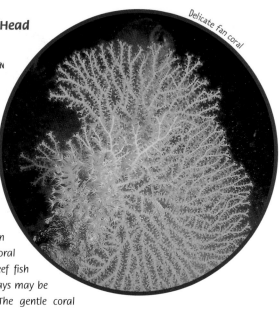

Delicate fan coral

Jazirat Al Khayl

OTHER NAME:	HORSE ISLAND
DIVE TYPE:	ROCK WALLS, FALLEN ROCK AND CORAL
DEPTH:	6M TO 40M+
GPS:	N 26° 22' 24" E 56° 26' 51"

The deeper north side of this island is dived from the headland in the east into the bays and along the north west headland. Steep cliffs and rock scree run sharply down into the sea to a coral covered shelf 6 metres deep. The boulder and coral slope steps down to a wide shelf at 25 to 30 metres, then drops on to the shelving sand at 40 metres. Lots of reef fish can be seen here and the occasional sharks keeping their distance.

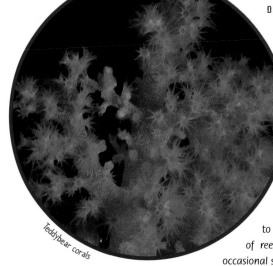

Teddybear corals

Ras Musandam

OTHER NAME:	WALL STREET
DIVE TYPE:	ROCK WALLS, FALLEN ROCK AND CORAL
DEPTH:	6M TO 40M+
GPS:	N 26°23'12" E 56°31'29"

This dive site is on the northern most point of Jazirat Musandam which is one of the largest islands in the Musandam. Along this coast of the island the high sheer cliffs drop straight down into the sea to a narrow ledge at 6 metres. They then drop steeply down to a wider shelf at 25 to 30 metres and on down to the shelving sand at 50 metres. This wall is scrubbed nearly bare of marine growth by the strong currents and makes an excellent drift dive. Sharks, dolphins and whale sharks are often seen drifting along this wall.

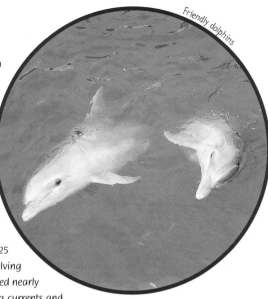

Friendly dolphins

Kachalu Island

OTHER NAME:	UNKNOWN
DIVE TYPE:	ROCK WALLS, FALLEN ROCK AND CORAL
DEPTH:	6M TO 40M+
GPS:	N 26°23'46" E 56°31'48"

Close up of soft leather coral

One of the more popular sites, which can be dived in moderate currents. The rock walls of the island drop straight down to a shelf at 5 metres, then step steeply down to 50 metres+. There are lots of gullies, holes and small shelves filled with hard and soft corals. One cave passes through the island and is nicknamed the "washing machine". Large shoals of fish frequent this site; several whale sharks have also been seen here.

Bu Rashid

OTHER NAME:	RASHID'S FATHER
DIVE TYPE:	ROCK WALLS, FALLEN ROCK AND CORAL
DEPTH:	6M TO 40M+
GPS:	N 26° 24' 12" E 56° 29' 42"

This is one of the larger islands in the Strait of Hormuz. The steep rocky cliffs drop down into the sea to a coral covered shelf at 6 metres and continue on down to a wide shelf at 25 to 30 metres before dropping on to the shelving sand at 40 metres. On the north side is a wreck of a small fiberglass boat and several species of shark are regularly seen here.

Zebra shark

Ruqq Suwayk

OTHER NAME:	CALCULATOR ROCK
DIVE TYPE:	ROCK SEAMOUNT CORAL REEF
DEPTH:	6M TO 50M+
GPS:	N 26° 24' 12" E 56° 28 42"

Black coral

This seamount can be seen just below the surface at 6 metres. The top of the mount is flat and covered with soft corals and several gullies are cut into the top of the rock. The sides step down in terraces to 50 metres+. On the west side, a trail of debris, calculators and cargo lead down to a wrecked dhow at 40 metres. Several types of shark can be seen here gliding up out of the depths or just circling the seamount.

Ennerdale Rock

OTHER NAME:	UNKNOWN
DIVE TYPE:	ROCK SEAMOUNT, AND CORALS
DEPTH:	16M TO 50M+
GPS:	N 26° 27' 40" E 56° 30' 57"

This spectacular site is named after a bulk carrier that sank upon striking the rock. The rock, quite difficult to find and to dive, is located in the main shipping channel where the currents can be fearsome, but well worth the effort. The rock peak rises very steeply up from the deep to a sharp point at 16 metres below the surface. We use a grappling hook on a shot line to get down to this rock, which glows out of the dark greeny blue as you dive towards it.

The first things you see are the huge giant trevally and jacks patrolling around the rock, then the bright corals. The fish here are completely unafraid of divers and get very close.

Jacks patroling for an easy meal

Cormorants sunning themselves

Fanaku Island

OTHER NAME:	GAP ISLAND
DIVE TYPE:	ROCK WALLS, BOULDERS, AND CORALS
DEPTH:	6M TO 50M+
GPS:	N 26° 29' 55" E 56° 31 50"

This island is in the middle of three islands in the centre of the Strait of Hormuz. The sparsely covered rock walls descend down in terraces. The currents can be very strong here and being a small island, there is no shelter from the currents, so only the small and strongest marine growth manage to survive. This is shark, jack and tuna territory and they can be seen on most dives.

Great Quion Island

OTHER NAME:	UNKNOWN
DIVE TYPE:	ROCK WALLS, LARGE BOULDERS, FALLEN ROCK AND CORAL
DEPTH:	6M TO 50M+
GPS:	N 26° 30' 21" E 56° 30' 52"

The northern-most island in the Oman, this is the largest of the three islands in the main channel of the Strait of Hormuz and offers protection from the currents. The west side is gradual shelving rock, coral and sand. The south and east side of the cliff walls drop straight into the sea and then run steeply down in terraces. The rocks and boulders on this side of the island are lightly covered in growth. From the northern point of the island a submerged narrow rocky ridge runs north east about 20 metres below the surface. Extending to 900 metres, this ridge drops very steeply to the west and is a favourite hunting ground for sharks, trevally and jacks.

Spotted sweetlips

Multi-storey staghorn coral

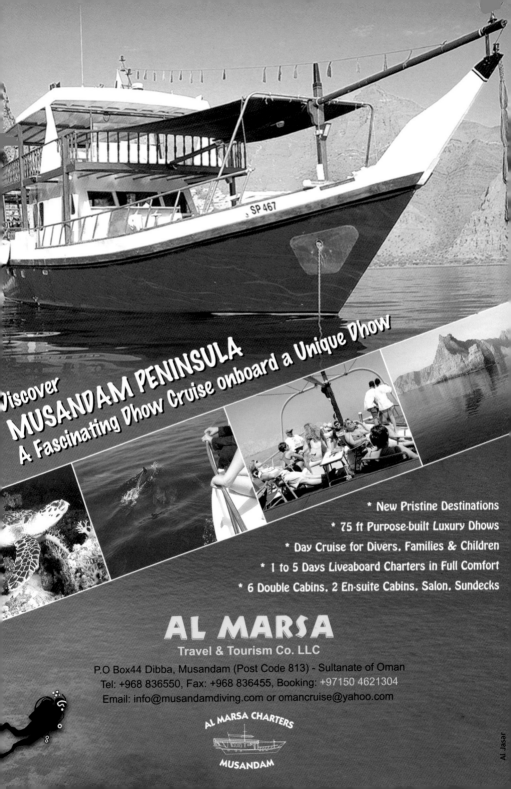

East Coast Dives

East Coast Overview Map

Arabian Gulf

Ras Al Khaimah

Dubai

Gulf of Oman

Fujairah

Hatta

Abd Dhabi

UAE

Al Ain

OMAN

Bayah Port Dibba

Dibba Island

Inchcape 1

Snoopy Island

Sharm Rocks

Car Cemetry

Lulaya Harbour

Shark Island/Khor Fakkan Island

Coral Gardens

Khor Fakkan Harbour

Anemone Gardens

Inchcape 2

Martini Rock

Ras Qidfa

- Harbours
- Dive sites (Covered)
- Dive sites (not covered)

Diving the East Coast

Diving on the East Coast is very different to diving in the Arabian Gulf; while the West Coast offers wrecks, the East Coast is the place for divers seeking tropical marine life. The East Coast is affected by currents from the Gulf of Oman, the Arabian Sea and the Indian Ocean. These bring a multitude of exotic fish and most resident divers in the UAE would agree that the greater diversity of marine life makes this the most interesting side of the peninsular to dive.

Depending on the moon's cycle, currents can sometimes be a problem, and dive operators will either anchor or carry out drift dives. The visibility is normally between 3-20 metres.

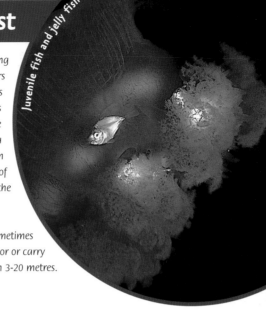

Juvenile fish and jelly fish host

Diver Safety

In order to make your East Coast dives safe and pleasant, keep in mind the following points.

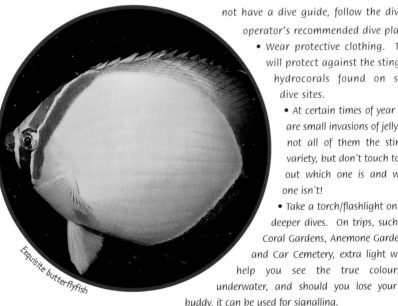

Exquisite butterflyfish

- If it's your first time on the site and you do not have a dive guide, follow the dive operator's recommended dive plan.
- Wear protective clothing. This will protect against the stinging hydrocorals found on some dive sites.
- At certain times of year there are small invasions of jellyfish – not all of them the stinging variety, but don't touch to find out which one is and which one isn't!
- Take a torch/flashlight on the deeper dives. On trips, such as Coral Gardens, Anemone Gardens and Car Cemetery, extra light will help you see the true colours underwater, and should you lose your buddy, it can be used for signalling.

- Buoyancy. At Car Cemetery in particular you need to be careful of your buoyancy. Caution is needed as this site tends to silt up quickly, so control your finning techniques to minimize stirring up the silt.

Night Diving

Night diving on the East Coast is very rewarding and you will find a lot of marine activity. At this time, a lot of creatures that are shy and sensitive to light come out to play, and to hunt and feed. Other creatures tuck themselves into rock crevices, hide in shells or cocoon themselves in a thin film 'sleeping blanket' to guard against being eaten.

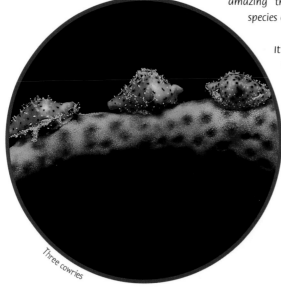

Octopus

At night, creatures also change colour to various shades of red in an attempt to camouflage themselves (red is the colour that is most difficult to see underwater at night). When we discover these creatures and shine our torch on them, we can see the true beauty of them in their red attire! This amazing transformation applies to many species of fish and octopus.

It's advisable to receive adequate training before your first night dive. We also suggest that you dive with a minimum of three torches between two divers (even better to have two torches each). Ensure you grease the rings correctly (if appropriate) and always use alkaline batteries for safety. Batteries never seem to last long underwater and torches are apt to flood

Three cowries

114

Anemone Gardens

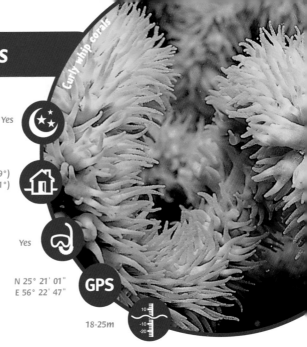

Curly whip corals

OTHER NAMES: —
DIVE TYPE: A LEVEL CORAL REEF

Yes

Lulaya Harbour 2.1nm @ 179° (359°)
Khor Fakkan Harbour 1.0 nm @ 081° (261°)

Yes

Details

There are many small sites within Anemone Gardens. All around Shark Island is a level coral reef, with a few metres depth differentiation in any direction. These sites are very pretty with plenty of green whip corals (actually a type of black coral).

N 25° 21' 01"
E 56° 22' 47" **GPS**

18-25m

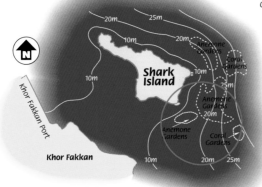

Diving

The best way to dive this area is with a compass and computer. Keeping an eye on your bottom times, explore the dive site searching for elusive sea horses, then make your way back to Shark Island. As the reef becomes shallower on your way to the island, you can have a safety stop, extend your dive time and admire the spectacular marine life.

Night Diving

This is an even more beautiful site to dive at night than in the daytime. The corals appear brighter by torchlight, and they will have their coral tentacles/polyps fully extended for feeding. If you are lucky, you may see sea horses with their tails wrapped around the corals, but look closely since they blend in with their background. You will also see moray eels swimming freely as they look for food. Look up occasionally; you may be fortunate enough to see squid. These are very inquisitive and attracted to light – they sometimes become dazzled and swim directly into the torch beam.

Squid at night

At night, it's almost impossible to dive this site and to locate the anchor line to ascend, so extra care needs to be taken. Always be aware of your depth, take a compass bearing and keep to the dive operator's recommended dive plan/time. The dive operator needs to be vigilant. It's best to anchor between Anemone Gardens and Shark Island, otherwise your time underwater will be further limited due to the depth.

Marine Life

It's common to see shoals of several species of fish congregating around the island – from jacks and juvenile barracuda to fusiliers and small schools of squid. You will find lots of beautiful hard and soft corals in a kaleidoscope of colours, the main ones being orange and red teddy bear corals and lots of wispy green whip corals swaying underwater.

This is an excellent dive spot, especially if you wish to see the elusive sea horse (please look carefully and DO NOT touch). Refer to Shark Island for details of other marine life.

Sea horse

Snorkelling

Snorkelling is possible, especially on days when the visibility is 20 metres plus. However, it's probably better to swim across to Shark Island instead. Refer to Shark Island for details on snorkelling.

Teddybear coral polyps

Cave corals

Car Cemetery

OTHER NAMES: —

DIVE TYPE: WRECKED CARS ON A SANDY SEABED

Yes

Lulaya Harbour 1.6nm @ 350° (170°)
Khor Fakkan Harbour 4nm @ 081° (261°)

No

N 25° 25' 07"
E 56° 22' 34" **GPS**

16-18m

Key

 Car

Truck

Nets over Vehicles

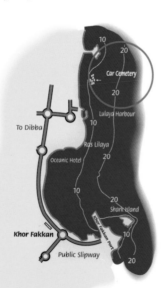

To Dibba

Lulaya Harbour

Ras Lilaya

Oceanic Hotel

Shark Island

Khor Fakkan

Public Slipway

Details

Car Cemetery is a graveyard for wrecked cars that was created in about 1988 to form an artificial reef and a special site for fishing. There are about 200 vehicles and the nucleus covers approximately 60 square metres.

Note that the map only depicts the main 'nucleus' of the car wrecks.

Diving

This is a difficult site to both find and navigate around, due to the flat seabed and the lack of any distinguishing features on the cars. Visibility is usually poor as this site is near a wadi entrance.

Most of the cars are covered with algae and fishing nets, some of which have fishing pots on them. There is a lot of sediment in the area, so take care to keep your buoyancy in check, otherwise you will be down to zero visibility!

Omani clingfish

Night Diving

Due to the 'openness' of the area, which is at the mercy of the wind and currents, this is a tricky site to navigate around at night, but not impossible. You will need to arrive in daylight and position yourself correctly, then wait for darkness.

In the daytime, you tend to meander from one wrecked car to another, looking in the distance for the shadow of the next vehicle, but at night you are unable to do this and you will need to rely on your compass. The dive operator should be prepared to up-anchor to collect you if you do not ascend the anchor rope.

Although not frequently dived in the dark, Car Cemetery makes a memorable night dive. Corals come out at night extending their polyps, feeding and catching micro-planktons. We have encountered several unusual nudibranchs, which are light sensitive and not seen in the daytime. There is also a beautiful sand anemone, which looks like the nondescript half of a tennis ball during the day, but at night extends itself to feed, resembling a bunch of celery decorated with

Sand anemone

baubles. Once a photo is taken the bright light of the flash from the strobe forces it to retract.

Marine Life

Since the visibility is usually poor, it's best to take your time and look for smaller creatures, such as shrimps and Omani clingfish hiding in the featherstars. This site is considered a nudibranch haven and you will find numerous species on the wrecks and discarded fishing nets. Look carefully for sea horses and frogfish, plus small manta rays and the occasional spotted eagle ray. There are also two large resident honeycomb morays on these wrecks, which are about 2 metres long.

Don't dismiss this site because of the low visibility; persevere, look closely, and you never know what you might find.

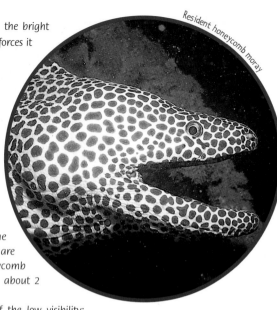

Resident honeycomb moray

Snorkelling

Snorkelling is poor due to low visibility.

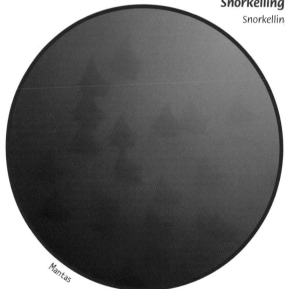

Mantas

Coral Gardens

OTHER NAMES: —

DIVE TYPE: A SOFT CORAL REEF ON A SANDY SEABED LOCATED ON THE NORTH-EASTERN SIDE OF SHARK ISLAND

Yes

Purple whip coral

Lulaya Harbour 2.1nm @ 179 (359°)
Khor Fakkan Harbour 1nm @ 081° (261°)

Details

No

Coral Gardens is one of the deepest sites on the East Coast and can be an interesting multi-level dive. It's difficult to locate unless you follow the correct bearings closely, but if you miss the exact location, no problem, just follow the compass bearing back to Shark Island and you will encounter smaller, shallower reefs on the way. The area is resplendent with green coloured black whip coral.

N 25° 21' 12"
E 56° 22' 48"

GPS

23m

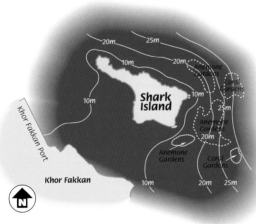

Khor Fakkan port

Shark Island

20m 25m
10m 20m Anemone Gardens
10m Coral Gardens
10m
25m
Anemone Gardens
20m
Anemone Gardens Coral Gardens

Khor Fakkan

10m 20m 25m

N

Diving

As this is a 'flat' site, we suggest that you follow one of the following two dive plans, preferably with a dive computer. The site is prone to both thermoclines and unusually strong currents. Do not attempt Dive Plan 2 if there is a strong current.

We suggest that this site is only suitable for more advanced divers with a minimum experience of 30 dives. It's sensible to have a spare cylinder for these deeper dives.

Dive Plan 1 Stay on the dive site, but watch your bottom time and give yourself a good safety stop.

Dive Plan 2 For a multi-level dive, explore this site for a maximum of 10-15 minutes (or according to the dive computer), then follow a compass bearing back to the island. You will find that your bottom time increases as you follow the reef up to 13 metres and arrive at the base of the island, usually within 30 minutes. This allows you more time to enjoy the actual site, as well as to have a good safety stop.

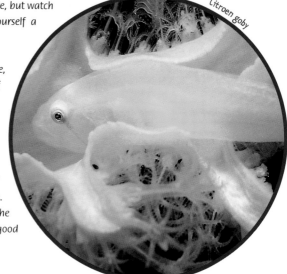
Citroen goby

Night Diving

Coral Gardens is a beautiful night dive. Corals are out feeding, nudibranchs hunting and molluscs, crayfish, lobsters and crabs are on the march at an incredible speed!

However, this is a deep night dive and fairly 'open', so adequate preparations and planning are vital. It's imperative that you take the time and depth into consideration and make any contingency plans prior to your dive. It can be tricky to find the anchor at night, but not impossible! One option in case of difficulty is to navigate your way over to Shark Island.

Dandelion coral

Marine Life

This location has some unusual soft corals that aren't seen on other dives. In particular, the delicate soft dandelion coral is fairly common here. There are also clumps of green wispy whip coral, swaying underwater – during the winter months, you may be lucky to see razorfish (also known as shrimpfish), swimming upside down and darting from one clump of coral to another. You may also see guitar sharks, and large crocodilefish, with their big flat heads, crocodile shaped mouths and beautiful eyes with frilly eyelids. Sea horses are seen occasionally, although they are becoming increasingly rare.

Snorkelling

This location is too deep to see anything from the surface, you are better off swimming across to Shark Island.

Shrimp on starfish

Dibba Island

OTHER NAMES: —

DIVE TYPE: **AN ISLAND WITH LONG SLOPING SIDES, COVERED IN HARD AND SOFT CORALS**

Yes

Lulaya Harbour 12.8nm @ 347° (167°)
Khor Fakkan Harbour 15.2nm @ 353° (173°)

Details

Yes

This small rocky island has long sloping sides that are covered by a reef of a variety of soft and boulder corals. The side nearest the shore should be dived at high tide, since the depth is a maximum of 3-4 metres. The seaward side has a long sloping rocky reef with many green and purple whip corals, making it a very pretty dive site. You are virtually guaranteed to see turtles here.

N 25° 36' 06"
E 56° 20' 05"

GPS

16m

Kurt, from the Holiday Beach Motel, has been very proactive in protecting Dibba Island and has placed several mooring buoys around the island. Please utilise these buoys, instead of dropping your anchor and spoiling the corals and reef growth.

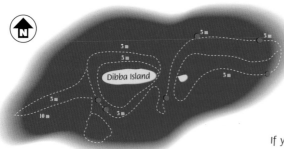

Dibba Island

● Buoys

Diving

If you are in a hurry, it's possible to complete a circuit around the island in one dive, but only at high tide. Regardless of the tide, it's a good idea if you are planning several dives in this area, to explore the wall, which runs parallel with the island. This area is prone to both thermoclines and unusual, strong currents.

Low Tide Keep to the north (seaward) side of the island, otherwise you'll be snorkelling, instead of diving, on the south (shore) side.

High Tide Explore the side of the island nearest the mainland. You may see turtles here.

Night Diving

Dibba Island makes a lovely, easy night dive, with no problems for navigation. There are lots of beautiful, swaying corals with their polyps fully extended for feeding. You will also find sleeping fish, which have lodged themselves between the rocks and boulders, often leaving their tails exposed.

Clownfish peeking out of its anemone host

You may also come across sleeping turtles (do not touch or disturb these creatures; they are easily alarmed and can swallow too much water and drown). If you don't disturb them, you will have longer to examine them close up – a wonderful experience!

Turtle

Marine Life

You will see many species of fish on this site, plus you are almost guaranteed to see turtles. Look out for the unusual jawfish (or hole goby), noticeable for their rather ugly features – huge heads and large eyes and mouths. They build a lovely 'drainpipe' home, the walls lined with pretty shells to prevent them from collapsing. The drainpipe goes down quite a long way and once the jawfish disappears into it, it takes a long time to reappear. When it's mating season (usually June - August, although it appears to depend on water temperatures), they pop out of their holes, exposing their beautiful, patterned and colourful bodies.

There are also lots of anemones with their resident clownfish; be careful of these little guys – they are sometimes rather aggressive and can bash your mask with quite a force or give you a nip or two!

Snorkelling

This is one of the best snorkelling sites around, especially for seeing turtles. The turtles are most prolific on the seaward side of the island where there are lots of coral reefs, and it seems that snorkellers will see turtles, even when divers don't.

Swim out to the island if you are a strong and proficient swimmer, otherwise go by boat for safety.

Jawfish at home

Jawfish during mating season

Inchcape 1

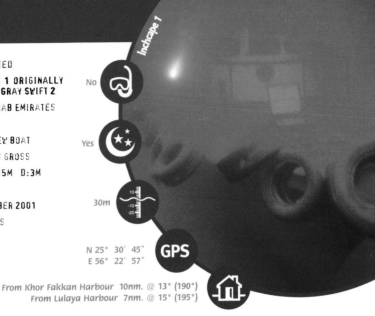

WRECK REGISTER: NOT CHARTED

NAME:	INCHCAPE 1 ORIGINALLY KNOWN AS GRAY SWIFT 2
NATIONALITY:	UNITED ARAB EMIRATES
YEAR BUILT:	1971
TYPE:	STEEL CREW BOAT
TONNAGE:	57 TONNES GROSS
DIMENSIONS:	L:21M B:5M D:3M
CARGO:	NONE
DATE SUNK:	12 DECEMBER 2001
CHARTED DEPTH:	30 METRES

No

Yes

30m

N 25° 30' 45"
E 56° 22' 57" **GPS**

From Khor Fakkan Harbour 10nm. @ 13° (190°)
From Lulaya Harbour 7nm. @ 15° (195°)

Circumstances of Loss

Sunk, by Inchcape Shipping Services to form an artificial offshore reef.

Details

The boat was built in the USA by Halter Marine and shipped to Dubai in 1971/1972. She started her service in Ras Al Khaimah and in 1991 moved to Dubai and was re-named Inchcape 1. Her working life was to support Inchcape Shipping Services transporting crew and supplies to and from ships and oil platforms and rigs in both Dubai and Fujairah. Decommisioned in 2001.

General Manager Eric Laing and his colleagues, Captain Joe Finch and Louise Marr of Inchcape Shipping Services decided that the decommissioned boat would be ideal to sink and form an artificial offshore reef. The engines were removed and cleaned of oil residues and the doors and hatches were taken off to allow divers to swim through. HRH Sheikh Hamed Bin Mohamed Al Sharqi granted permission for this boat to be sunk and with the assistance of Dibba Municipality, Sandy Beach Motel, Sandy Beach Dive Centre, Al Boom and Inchcape Shipping Services, the boat was relocated to her final resting place.

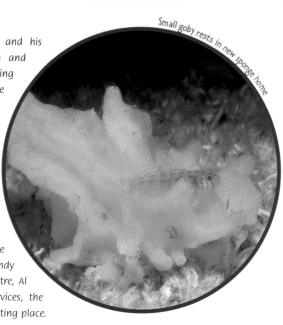

Small goby rests in new sponge home

Diving

This is a small vessel, sitting upright with car tyres still in place around the gunwales and a couple of the hatches can be found on the sea bed at the stern of the wreck.

The depth of this dive is over 30 meters depending on the tide. The wreck is small and it is possible to go around it several times during a dive, the best way is to swim slowly, starting from the seabed. After searching for the many residents hiding between the hull and seabed, ascend to the deck area where you can explore the holds and the engine room. You will need a light to reveal the marine life seeking the sanctuary of these dark spaces and with a bit of a squeeze, access into the wheelhouse is possible. You can then go up to the top of the wheelhouse and on to the navigation mast to enjoy the last few minutes before ascending.

Shoals of fish mob the wreck

Marine Life

Although this is a relatively new wreck site, the "fish world" took up residence very rapidly. You can already find large rays hiding under the wreck towards the stern. There is a large shoal of cardinal fish taking up all the space in the safety of the wheelhouse, attempting to avoid being eaten by the large barracuda and emperor fish cruising outside waiting for an easy meal.

The Navigation Box Blenny

You will see large hammour and several species of moray eels hiding in the tyres. Look out for yellow-mouthed moray, pennant fish, box fish, soldier fish and red bigeyes. The fish life is attracted by the spreading algae. There is a large resident blenny sitting in the navigation box and if you look closely you will see many species of nudibranchs. There are more and more fish beginning to congregate on this wreck and you never know what you might find!

Safety

This is a fairly deep site: 30 metres and the currents can be quite strong.

Shoal of red bigeyes

Inchcape 2

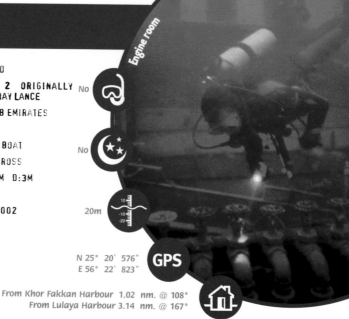

WRECK REGISTER: NOT CHARTED

NAME: INCHCAPE 2 ORIGINALLY KNOWN AS GRAY LANCE

NATIONALITY: UNITED ARAB EMIRATES

YEAR BUILT: 1974

TYPE: STEEL CREW BOAT

TONNAGE: 58 TONNES GROSS

DIMENSIONS: L:24M B:6M D:3M

CARGO: NONE

DATE SUNK: APRIL 24, 2002

CHARTED DEPTH: 20 METRES

No

No

20m

N 25° 20' 576"
E 56° 22' 823"

GPS

From Khor Fakkan Harbour 1.02 nm. @ 108°
From Lulaya Harbour 3.14 nm. @ 167°

Circumstances of Loss

Sunk by Inchcape Shipping Services to form an artificial offshore reef. This is the second ship the company has dedicated to a marine habitat. See Inchcape 1 details.

Details

The boat was built in the USA by Halter Marine and shipped to Dubai on a Hansa Line vessel in 1974.

She started her service in Dubai and was moved to Fujairah during 1991. She was renamed in 1993 and eventually relocated to Ras Al Khaimah in 1995. She transported crew and supplies to and from ships, oil platforms and rigs during her working life.

Although she had recently received a completely new coat of paint, it was found that she needed considerably more work to make her seaworthy, so the decision was made to decommission her.

The artificial reef created when Inchcape 1 was sunk was so successful and the marine life it attracted in a relatively short time was so prolific that it inspired the Inchcape team, Eric Laing, Captain Joe Finch and Louise Marr to offer Inchcape 2 for the same purposes. The wreck was sunk in shallower waters to give access to the majority of divers.

Corals encrusting the decks

The boat was moved from Ras Al Khaimah to Fujairah Port and was prepared for her new life underwater. It took more than two weeks to ensure she was cleaned of oil residues; the doors and hatches were taken off to enable divers to swim through the wreck safely.

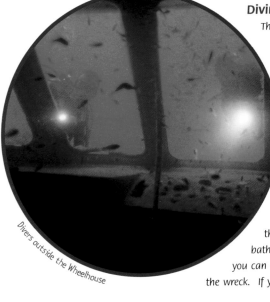
Divers outside the Wheelhouse

Diving

The Inchcape 2 sits upright in 20 meters with the bow facing 90°. You can find debris around the wreck, the engine hatch doors, other doors and a few shattered glass windows from the wheelhouse, which were pushed out with pressure as the wreck was sinking.

You can enter and swim through the whole wreck end-to-end. Entry can be gained through the aft deck hatches to the engine room. Swim through the living quarters, past the bathroom and when you've seen enough, you can exit through stairs at either side of the wreck. If you are more adventurous and of medium build, you can exit through the bow hatchway. Take care if you choose this route; while it is quiet easy and safe, ensure your equipment dosen't get snagged.

Loading marks

The best way to enjoy this wreck is to go down the buoy line, currently connected to the port side of the stern. Move slowly around the wreck and explore the sea-bed; you will find some large jawfish hiding amongst the debris strewn around. You may be able to see the loading marks with numbers on the bow, although these are fast becoming encrusted with calcerous worms and various algae and bryozoans. Once around the wreck, ascend to the deck area, through the engine room and along to the bow. Alternatively, you can look in from the outside. Shine your torch inside the engine room and you will find lots of juveniles hiding between the engine parts and pipes. The wheelhouse is spacious and you can easily enter and exit through the gaping holes.

White anemones

Marine Life

The wreck is located between Martini Rock and Anemone Gardens. The abundant fish life of these two sites has spread quickly to occupy this new habitat. Already there are rays, moray eels, juvenile barracuda, jacks and cardinals benefiting from this new wreck. During the initial months the wreck was covered with small white anemones, which carpeted the decks and railings, giving the wreck a "ghostly" glow. Various sponges, young teddybear corals, encrusting worms and algae have also rapidly taken over the wreck and are enjoying their new home.

Martini Rock

Teddybear corals

OTHER NAMES: —

DIVE TYPE: CORAL REEFS,
SHELVING SANDY
BOTTOM AND DROP-OFFS

Yes

Lulaya Harbour 3.3nm @ 179° (359°)
Khor Fakkan Harbour 1.3nm @ 122° (302°)

Yes

Details

Martini Rock is a small, submerged coral outcrop, the top of which is visible from the surface at 3 metres. The rock has several sandy gullies or alleys and most of it is covered in orange and purple teddybear coral, creating a pleasing and colourful dive site.

N 25° 20' 05"
E 56° 22' 53"

GPS

3-22m

Martini Rock

This is an excellent site for all levels of diver and a favourite location on the East Coast.

Diving

The north side of the rock is the deepest, going down to 22 metres, while all other areas are shallower at about 13 metres. There's enough time to complete a circuit of the rock in one dive, but note that the site is prone to both thermoclines and unusual, strong currents.

The variety of fish life is excellent and the top 5 metres are like an aquarium – schools of snapper, fusiliers, anthias, triggerfish and large-mouth mackerel are present for most of the year.

Night Diving

Excellent for night dives, although if you don't know the site well, navigation may be a problem. You may see sleeping turtles, rays out feeding and perhaps a spotted eagle ray.

The rock appears completely red because of all the feeding teddybear corals. Look closely into the soft corals to find fish, such as juvenile damselfish or hawkfish, which use the coral as a safe haven from larger fish that are out looking for dinner. If you stay near the bottom of the rock on the seabed, you may see large rays sifting through the sand feeding on small molluscs and crustaceans. They will come right up to you; it can cause quite a scare!

Hawkfish

You may also encounter large pufferfish, which swim about at night completely oblivious of their surroundings, bumping around rather like a ball in a pinball machine! Don't shine your torch at them for too long, otherwise they will be completely disorientated!

On a few night dives, we were fortunate to encounter some strange looking fish called long finned waspfish (a type of gurnard). They appear to run over the seabed on three spider-like legs, which are hidden underneath their winged fins. They have two pronged feelers extending from their mouths, which they use to search for creatures hidden in the silty seabed.

Long finned waspfish

Marine Life

Large sections of the rock are covered in red, purple and orange teddybear corals, on one side it is swathed in purple whip corals and in a deep corner there are green and white whip corals. There are also clumps of featherstars, hiding shrimps, Omani clingfish, and sometimes nudibranchs.

You may be fortunate to see the occasional leopard shark, black tip reef shark and/or a guitar shark. We have also found some unusual creatures; a pygmy seamoth, frogfish and a robust pipefish. The sight of these unusual tropical creatures here in the UAE caused great excitement.

Beware during the mating season of the red tooth triggerfish (June, July, August). It tends to dart towards you at a fast pace, only to turn away at the last moment with millimetres to spare. They are guarding their territory, so heed their warning and swim by quickly!

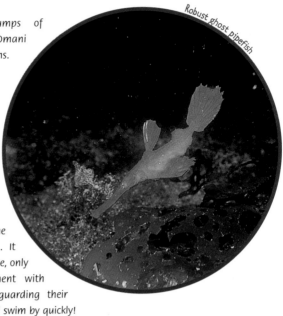

Robust ghost pipefish

Snorkelling

This is another good, rocky, shallow location which is teeming with fish life and is a favourite with snorkellers. The top of the rock is around 2-3 metres from the surface (depending on the tide), and the bright colours of the teddybear corals decorating the rock are easily seen. You may also see shoals, boxfish, jacks and many shoals of fish near the surface. If you can duck dive down to 5 metres or more, you may see morays, rays and perhaps a turtle.

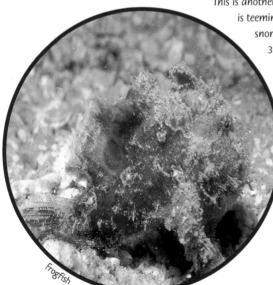

Frogfish

Ras Qidfa

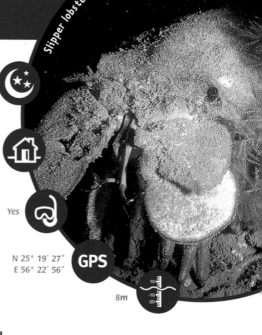

Slipper lobster

OTHER NAMES: —

DIVE TYPE: SMALL HEADLAND LEADING
INTO THE BAY AT MARTINI
ROCK

Yes

Khor Fakkan Harbour 2.1nm @ 204° (024°)
Lulaya Harbour 4.9nm @ 201° (021°)

Details

Leading into Martini Rock bay, Ras
Qidfa is a small, rocky headland where
you will find many hard corals and rocky
boulders.

Yes

N 25° 19' 27"
E 56° 22' 56"

GPS

8m

To Dibba

Ras Lulaya

Oceanic Hotel

10

20

10

20

Shark Island

Khor
Fakkan
Port

Khor Fakkan

Public Slipway

To Fujairah

10

20

Martini
Rock

10

Ras Qidfa

Qidfa

Diving

It's best to start the dive at the southern end of Ras
Qidfa, and travel north, heading towards Martini
Rock bay, and keeping the rocks, boulders and
wall on your left-hand side. There's plenty to see,
including a multitude of species of fish, turtles
and hard and soft corals. However, it's less
interesting if you leave the rocky shores and
venture onto the sandy seabed.

Night Diving

This is a pleasant and easy spot for night
diving. Simply follow the wall, keeping it on
your left, and look in the nooks and crannies
in the rocks for banded shrimp, slipper
lobsters and crayfish. There are not as many
corals here as on other sites, but you may be
rewarded with glimpses of sleeping turtles,
rays or even spotted eagle rays.

Marine Life

There is plenty of fish life to see here; species include fusiliers, jacks and triggerfish. There are also soft and hard corals with polyps out feeding. Look out for turtles and crayfish. Look in the featherstars for small shrimps and squat lobsters which are camouflaged by changing their colour to match their featherstar hosts.

Squat lobster in featherstar

Snorkelling

This is a good spot for snorkellers, especially if you enjoy the marine life on the seabed. It's a shallow site, and you will see most by staying close to the shoreline, rather than venturing further out where there are only moses sole, (although with luck you might see rays and turtles).

Shrimp in featherstar

Shark Island

OTHER NAMES: KHOR FAKKAN ISLAND

DIVE TYPE: ISLAND WITH SLOPING SIDES, COVERED IN HARD AND SOFT CORALS

Yes

Lulaya Harbour 2.4nm @ 183° (003°)
Khor Fakkan Harbour 1nm @ 081° (261°)

Yes

Details

This fairly large island stands proud at the south-eastern end of the magnificent Khor Fakkan bay. It has a great beach for picnics, to dive and snorkel from, or to simply spend a relaxing day in the sun.

N 25° 21' 12"
E 56° 22' 36" **GPS**

16m

Diving

The depth around the island varies from a shallow 3-5 metres on the coastal side, becoming deeper towards the seaward side. The bottom is sandy and rocky, with a variety of hard and soft corals. The island can be dived from its beach, but most divers are dropped off at either Coral Gardens or Anemone Gardens, and complete the latter part of the dive close to the island. Diving or swimming around the whole island is not possible in one dive.

On the south-west tip of the island is a site known as Shark Drift. This is best dived starting at the deeper seaward-most point, where the bottom begins at 16 metres. Drift with the slight current and swim west around the island.

Warning Be aware that the rocks are covered with sea urchins, and, at certain times of the year, with small brown swimming anemones, which give a nasty sting if touched.

Night Diving

This is an excellent and very easy site for a night dive and any part of the island is accessible to be explored. There's usually lots of fish life, including sleeping turtles in the rocky overhangs. You may also find large, tail-less rays. These inquisitive creatures are wonderfully graceful, appearing like flying saucers in outer space. The rays are often covered in several remoras that attach themselves by their heads, which have a sucker-disc surface.

Pufferfish

Be careful of discarded fishing nets, especially at night. If you do get tangled up in one, stay still, do not panic and signal to your buddy for help. The island is also covered with lots of black urchins, which come out at night, so take care with your buoyancy to avoid painful punctures or injuries!

Marine Life

As the name suggests, this is a good place for sharks; in particular, blacktip reef sharks can be seen between November and April on the eastern point of the island. On the seabed you may see cerianthid anemones, pretty purple or white fronds sticking out of a cardboard looking tube. Don't disturb or touch, otherwise

Tube anemone/cerianthid

they retract down into their tubes. This area is the haunt of many schools of fish, from batfish and juvenile barracuda to big mouth mackerel, plus there are pufferfish, large rays with remoras and the occasional spotted eagle ray, which can be found in shallower water. During the winter months, you may sometimes see murex shells laying their straw-like eggs under the rocks.

Pineapple fish

Snorkelling

Snorkelling is sometimes better than diving here and the waters are shallow enough to be able to see the seabed from the surface. The whole coastline is good to explore, but if you want to see sharks, stay at the south-western corner of the island.

During the winter months you are more likely to see blacktip reef sharks swimming in the shallow waters at 1-3 metres. You can also find lots of hard and soft corals, turtles and, if the visibility is good, rays.

Blacktip reef sharks

Sharm Rocks

OTHER NAMES: THREE ROCKS, PINNACLES, ROCK PILES

DIVE TYPE: SEVERAL SMALL, LOW-LYING ROCKY MOUNDS, COVERED IN HARD AND SOFT CORALS

Yes

Lulaya Harbour 5.2nm @ 348° (168°)
Khor Fakkan Harbour 8.7nm @ 353° (173°)

Yes

N 25° 28' 55"
E 56° 21' 57" **GPS**

14m

Details

Not far from Snoopy Rock and the Sandy Beach Motel are these four small outcrops of rock, just breaking the surface of the water. They are covered in masses of soft corals and there is a small table coral reef towards the shore in about 4 metres of water. Note that navigation can be difficult here, as the small sandy gullies or alleys can be misleading and disorientating.

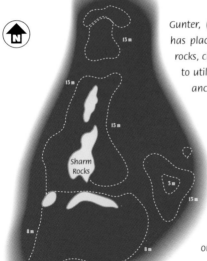

Gunter, (former owner of the Sandy Beach Dive Centre) has placed two mooring buoys on the north side of the rocks, close to the deepest part of the site. It's a good idea to utilise these buoys, rather than throwing in your own anchor and damaging the reef.

Diving

It's possible to complete a circuit of these rocks in one dive, although it's a bit of a rush, even in 60 minutes. The seaward side of the rocks is a vertical rocky wall, which goes down to 14 metres, while the shore side has a shallow table coral reef to one side and boulder coral outcrops on the other.

141

Night Diving

This is another excellent shallow site for night dives, but take your time, as it is crammed with marine life. Peep into the corals for fish seeking protection from the night hunters. You will also find lots of sleeping parrotfish, broomtailed wrasse and sometimes sleeping turtles.

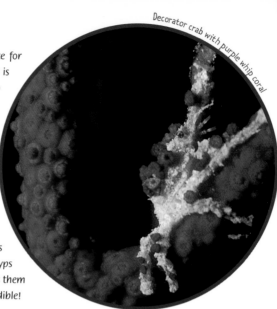
Decorator crab with purple whip coral

If you look hard, you may find a piece of moving coral attached to a sandy, dusty looking crab. This is a decorator crab and there are many different species here. The crab steals pieces of coral polyps from the main coral colony and attaches them to its own body for camouflage – incredible!

Marine Life

These rocks are full of shoals of fish; jacks, big mouth mackerel, fusiliers and sometimes squid. You may also see turtles, morays, crayfish and guitar sharks. Explore the bottom for moses soles – their mottled scales are excellent camouflage against the seabed. The only give-away being tiny flecks of gold that reflect from their bodies.

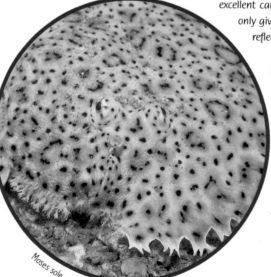
Moses sole

During the mating season (early evening at the beginning of the warmer months), you can see the strange and beautiful mating habits of boxfish and cuttlefish. At this time look out for the small, but fierce, anemone fish defending their anemone host, which is hiding and protecting its brood of eggs.

Snorkelling

The variety of fish life makes Sharm Rocks a very special location for snorkellers, and for some reason the parrotfish, boxfish and broomtailed wrasse appear to be larger here. All of these fish are visible when snorkelling and you may also see rays and turtles.

If you are a strong and proficient swimmer, it's possible to swim out to the rocks from the mainland in about ten minutes (depending on the weather), but hire a dive boat if you tire easily.

Large red crab

Boxfish

Snoopy Island

OTHER NAMES: JAZIRAT AL GHUBBAH

DIVE TYPE: ISLAND WITH SLOPING SIDES, FULL OF HARD CORALS   Yes

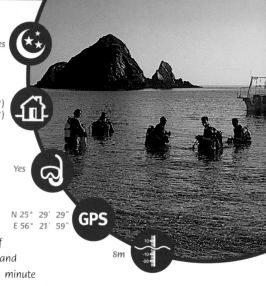

Lulaya Harbour 5.5nm @ 350° (170°)
Khor Fakkan Harbour 8nm @ 359° (179°)

Yes

Details

Allegedly named because it's shaped like Snoopy lying on his back with his nose in the air, the slopes of this small island are covered by several varieties of hard coral, home to a wealth of anemones and clownfish. At high tide, it's a good 10 minute swim to the edge of the island. However, during November there are unusually high and low tides, which make it possible to walk to the island without getting wet!

N 25° 29' 29"
E 56° 21' 59"   **GPS**

8m

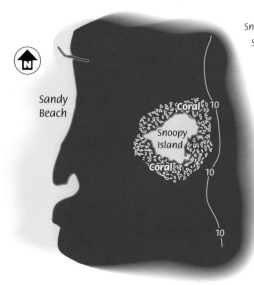

Sandy Beach

Coral 10

Snoopy Island

Coral 10

10

Snoopy Island can be visited from the Sandy Beach Motel. Divers can go to the dive operator, hire equipment and use their facilities. If you do not hire equipment and you have some non-divers, you will be charged beach entrance fees. In an attempt to protect its guests, the motel prohibits boats and jet skis from using the waters around Snoopy Island. However, occasionally boats still frequent the area between the island and the shore, so take care.

Diving

Snoopy Island is the only shore dive on the East Coast, making it one of the easiest (and most affordable) dives, since you do not have to rely on someone to operate a dive boat. Put your fins on in waist high water then swim a little further out before descending.

The southern side of the island offers the more interesting diving. Here there is plenty to see, including varied and plentiful marine life, several species of hard and soft corals and anemones.

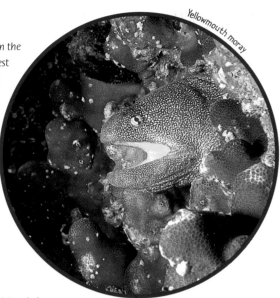

Yellowmouth moray

Night Diving

The trip from the shore to the island is very interesting; look out for sleeping fish, as well as starfish, sand dollars, crabs and molluscs, all busy looking for a tasty evening meal. You will also see shrimps, but only because their eyes shine out from the sand.

When you arrive at the rocks and corals at the base of the island, we suggest you turn right, keeping the island on your left. You will encounter many sleeping fish, morays and the occasional barracuda. There are also a few anemones with sleeping clownfish. Sometimes the anemones completely close up, resembling a huge, blue plastic bag!

Carole was almost chased out of the water by a lionfish on one night dive here when she persisted in taking a few too many photos of it!

Lionfish

Marine Life

There's a lot of marine life to see in this area, although there's less coral on the shore side of the island than on the seaward side. Among a variety of underwater life, you can expect to see big mouth mackerel, morays, anemones, clownfish and lionfish. Divers may also occasionally see turtles and sharks. Also look out for smaller marine life, pipefish, shrimps, crabs, and nudibranchs

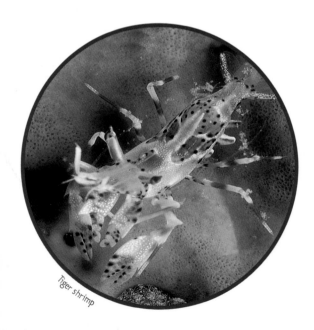

Pipefish hiding between murex shell eggs

Snorkelling

Snoopy Island is the easiest East Coast location for snorkellers to access and is relatively protected from all weather, except exceptionally heavy seas. The site is popular and on weekends can be rather busy. It is also a very shallow site, enabling you to see all the marine life mentioned above, as well as rays. However, a bonus for snorkellers is that they are more likely than divers to encounter the guitar sharks and blacktip sharks which appear during the cooler months.

Tiger shrimp

Sandy Beach

A DIVER'S HAVEN

Located on the Indian Ocean, in Fujairah, Sandy Beach offers the very best in diving facilities and equipment. Managed by a team of professional instructors (both NAUI & PADI), the Center conducts 3 daily boat dives at 9:30 a.m., 12:00 noon and 2:30 p.m. Shore dives are also available.

We welcome divers from any recognized certifying organization (NAUI, PADI, BSAC, CMAS, SSI, etc.).

Main Features of Our Center:

- Year-round diving
- Snoopy Island, our house reef, is both a snorkeler's and diver's paradise
- A well stocked dive shop featuring Scubapro, Uwatec, and Ikelite products
- Air filling up to 300 bars
- Mixed gas facility (nitrox)
- NAUI & PADI dive courses, open water to divemaster. No minimum students
- Pool & open water facilities on site
- Musandam safaris
- Motel rooms, chalets & bungalows, including a restaurant and bar
- Courteous customer service

Sandy Beach Diving Center
P.O. Box 659, Fujairah, U.A.E.

Tel: (+971 9) 244 5050   **Fax:** (+971 9) 244 5900   **E-mail:** sbdiving@emirates.net.ae

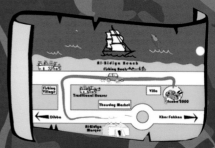

Pearls of Wisdom

UAE Overview

Visitors to the United Arab Emirates (UAE) will find a land of startling contrasts, from endless stretches of desert to rugged mountains and modern towns, edged by the glittering waters of the Arabian Gulf and the Gulf of Oman. This young country was created when seven emirates (i.e. states) joined together in 1971 to form the United Arab Emirates. The members are Abu Dhabi (the capital), Ajman, Dubai, Fujairah, Ras Al Khaimah, Sharjah and Umm Al Quwain. Each emirate is named after its main town.

Geography

Lying at the north-eastern part of the Arabian Peninsula, the United Arab Emirates (UAE) is bordered by the Kingdom of Saudi Arabia to the south and west, and the Sultanate of Oman to the east and north. It has a coastline on both the Gulf of Oman and the Arabian Gulf and is south of the strategically important Strait of Hormuz. The total area of the country is about 83,600 square kilometers.

Much of the region consists of desert and flat sabkha (salt-flats). In the western part of the country is the infamous Rub Al Khali or Empty Quarter desert – the largest sand desert in the world. However, to the east rise the dramatic Hajar Mountains (the word 'hajar' is the Arabic for rock). The highest point in the UAE is Jebel Yibir at 1,527 metres.

History

Less than 50 years ago, much of the region that is now the UAE was little more than empty desert and mountains, rarely visited and inhabited by a few Bedouin tribes and a sprinkling of villages and towns in the more hospitable areas.

However, with the discovery of oil the region was on its way to becoming the immensely wealthy and modern country that it is today.

Before this period, little had changed for centuries for the people who derived their livelihood from trade, fishing, pearling and small-scale agriculture. The Islamic faith appeared in 635 AD when a huge battle was fought on the East Coast at Dibba, (this is the moment that traditionally marks the Peninsula's conversion to Islam). From then on, various outside powers came to influence the region, including Oman, Portugal, Persia and finally Britain. By 1892 the individual rulers had accepted the protection of the British in the culmination of a series of maritime truces. In Europe, the area became known as the Trucial Coast (or Trucial States), a name it retained until the creation of the UAE in 1971. In 1968 Britain announced its withdrawal from the region and work began to try to create a single state consisting of Bahrain, Qatar and the Trucial Coast. Negotiations collapsed when Bahrain and Qatar chose to become independent states. However, the Trucial Coast remained committed to forming an alliance and in 1971 the Federation of the United Arab Emirates was created.

Under the agreement, the individual emirates each retained a degree of autonomy. The leaders of the new federation elected the Ruler of Abu Dhabi, HH Sheikh Zayed bin Sultan Al Nahyan, as their new president, a position he has held ever since.

The formation of the UAE came after the discovery of huge oil reserves (an estimated 9% of the world's known resources) in Abu Dhabi in 1958. While the other emirates have also struck oil, the finds have never been as extensive as in Abu Dhabi. However, the oil revenue allowed the development of an economic and social infrastructure, which is the basis of today's modern society. Much of the credit for this development can be traced to the vision of President HH Sheikh Zayed bin Sultan Al Nahyan.

Climate

The UAE has a sub-tropical, arid climate. Sunny blue skies and warm weather can be expected most of the year. Rainfall is infrequent and irregular, falling mainly in winter.

Temperatures range from a low of about 15°C (59°F) to a high of 48°C (118°F). The mean daily maximum is 24°C (75.2°F) in January rising to 41°C (105.8°F) in July.

Flora & Fauna

As you would expect in a country with such an arid climate, the variety of flora and fauna in the UAE isn't as extensive as in other parts of the world. However, a surprising number of creatures and plant life have managed to adapt themselves to life with high temperatures and little rainfall.

Most towns in the Emirates have an extensive greening programme underway. Areas along the roads are incredibly colourful for a desert environment, and there are also attractive and well-kept parks.

The date palm is the most widely known of the indigenous flora, but on the plains near the

JUST ADD AIR

THE COMPLETE DIVING EXPERIENCE

Aqua Centre, Dubai

- ▶ PADI Diving Courses.
- ▶ Largest Diveshop in the UAE.
- ▶ Service centre.
- ▶ Air Filling while you wait.
- ▶ On site training pool.
- ▶ Special courses for children.
- ▶ Friendly & professional staff.
- ▶ Refresher courses for the rusty diver.
- ▶ Pop in for a coffee and a chat.

The only dive centre in the UAE with a purpose built on site training pool

Oceanic Hotel, Khorfakkan

- ▶ Boat and shore diving.
- ▶ Oman day diving trips.
- ▶ Fully stocked dive and surf shop.
- ▶ Service centre.
- ▶ Air filling to 300 bar while you wait.
- ▶ PADI diving courses.
- ▶ Diving packages including accommodation available

Aqua Centre, Dubai, Tel: (04) 342-2993
Oceanic Dive Centre, Oceanic Hotel, Khorfakkan, Tel: (09) 237-0299

mountains flat topped Acacia trees and wild grasses give the impression of an African 'savannah'. In places the deserts are surprisingly green, even during the summer.

Indigenous fauna includes the Arabian leopard and the ibex, but sightings of them are extremely rare. Realistically, the only large animals you will see are camels and goats, (often roaming dangerously close to roads). Other desert life includes the sand cat, sand fox and desert hare, plus gerbils, hedgehogs, snakes and geckos.

Off the coast, the seas contain a rich abundance of marine life, including tropical fish, jellyfish, coral, the dugong ('sea cow'), dolphins, whales and sharks. A variety of breeds of turtle are also indigenous to the area, these include the loggerhead, hawksbill and the green turtle, all of which are under threat from man. The best known local fish is hammour, which is a type of grouper – it can be found on most restaurant menus!

Government & Ruling Family

The Supreme Council of Rulers is the highest authority in the UAE, comprising the hereditary Rulers of the seven emirates. The seven Rulers elect the chief of state (the President) from among its members.

The President of the UAE is HH Sheikh Zayed bin Sultan Al Nahyan who is also Ruler of Abu Dhabi. The Supreme Council also elects the Vice President, who is HH Sheikh Maktoum bin Rashid Al Maktoum, Ruler of Dubai.

International Relations

In its foreign relations the UAE's stance is one of non-alignment, but it is committed to the support of Arab unity. The country became a member of the United Nations and the Arab League in 1971. It is a member of the International Monetary Fund, the Organisation of Petroleum Exporting Countries (OPEC), the World Trade Organisation and other international and Arab organisations, including the Arab Gulf Co-operation Council (AGCC, also known as the GCC), whose other members are Bahrain, Kuwait, Oman, Qatar and Saudi Arabia.

Economy

The UAE has an open economy with one of the world's highest per capita incomes. Its wealth is chiefly based on the oil sector, which has been crucial to its development since the late 1960's. However, for 1999, 74% of total gross domestic product is from the non-oil sector.

Population

According to the Ministry of Planning, the population of the UAE stood at 2,377,453 in 1995. The mid year population estimate for 1999 puts the total number of nationals and expat residents at 2,938,000.

National Flag

The national flag consists of three equal horizontal bands, of green at the top, white and black at the bottom. A thicker vertical band of red runs down the hoist side.

Local Time

The UAE is four hours ahead of UCT (Universal Co-ordinated Time). There is no summer time saving when clocks are altered. When it's 12:00 midday in the UAE it's 08:00 in London; 13:30 in Delhi and 17:00 in Tokyo (not allowing for summer time saving in those countries).

Culture & Lifestyle

The UAE's culture is firmly rooted in the Islamic traditions of Arabia. Islam is more than just a religion, it is a way of life that governs even the minutiae of everyday events, from what to wear, to what to eat and drink.

Among the most highly prized virtues are courtesy and hospitality and visitors are sure to be charmed by the genuine warmth and friendliness of the people. Visitors will find a tolerant and welcoming country; foreigners are free to practice their own religion, alcohol is available, the dress code is liberal and women face little discrimination.

Language

The official language of the country is Arabic, although English, Urdu and Hindi are spoken and, with some perseverance, understood! All road and shop signs, restaurant menus etc., are in Arabic and English.

Religion

Islam is the official religion of the UAE, but other religions are respected and followers are allowed to practice their beliefs here.

Islam The basis of Islam is the belief that there is only one God and that Prophet Mohammed (Peace Be Upon Him), is his messenger. There are five pillars of the faith, which all Muslims must follow. One of which is the 'Hajj' or pilgrimage to the holy city of Mecca in Saudi Arabia.

Additionally a Muslim is required to pray to Mecca five times a day. The times vary according to the position of the sun. Friday is the holy day.

Ramadan In Islam, Ramadan is the holy month in which Muslims commemorate the revelation of the Holy Koran. It is a time of fasting when Muslims abstain from all food and drink, cigarettes and unclean thoughts between dawn and dusk. In the evening, fasting is broken with the Iftar feast.

Non-Muslims are also required to refrain from eating, drinking or smoking in public places during this time as a sign of respect. Independent restaurants and fast food outlets are closed during the day, although some offer take-aways. Hotels vary in their approach; most serve food indoors during the day, although this may only be to hotel guests. The sale of alcohol is limited to night time in outlets that have a special license.

Public Holidays

Islamic holidays are based on the Hijri calendar which is controlled by the sighting of the moon. As a result the dates of holidays are often confirmed less than 24 hours in advance. However, some non-Muslim holidays, such as UAE National Day on 2 December, are fixed according to the Gregorian calendar.

Social & Business Hours

Social hours are Mediterranean in style – in general people get up early, often have an afternoon siesta and eat late in the evening. Business and shop hours vary, but are based around the split-shift (closing for the early afternoon), or the straight shift (working straight through). Shops usually close at 10pm or midnight, and on Fridays places close for Prayer Time (11:30 - 13:30).

Clothing

While Emirati's wear their national dress, visitors are free to wear pretty much want they want, although a healthy amount of respect for local sensibilities doesn't go amiss. Dubai has a more liberal, relaxed approach, however, in the smaller emirates or on the East Coast you may prefer to be more discreet in your choice of attire. Lightweight summer clothing is suitable for most of the year, but something slightly warmer may be needed in the evening for the winter months, or when visiting air conditioned outlets. During the day, good quality sunglasses, hats and buckets of suncream are needed to avoid the lobster look!

Photography

Normal tourist photography is acceptable, but like anywhere in the world, it is courteous to ask permission before photographing people, especially local women. A wide choice of film is available.

Electricity & Water

The electricity supply is 220/240 volts and 50 cycles. The socket type is the same as the three point British plug and socket system.

The tap water is safe to drink, but most people prefer the locally bottled mineral water.

Arabic Cuisine

Modern Arabic cuisine is a blend of many types of cooking, from Moroccan, Tunisian, Iranian, Egyptian to Afghani, but in Dubai modern 'Arabic cuisine' invariably means Lebanese food. Typical ingredients include beef, lamb, chicken, rice, nuts (mainly pistachios), dates, honey, yoghurt and a range of seafood and spices.

Meat In Islam it is forbidden to consume the meat of any animal which has not been slaughtered in the correct manner. The meat of animals killed in accordance with the Islamic code is known as 'halal'.

In addition, pork is not included on the Arabic menu. Do not underestimate how taboo this meat is to a Muslim. It is not just in eating pork, but also in preparing and serving the meat. Images of pigs can also cause offence.

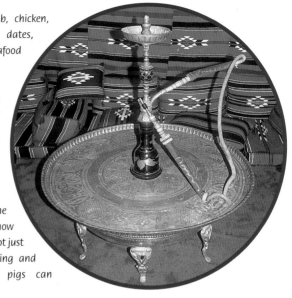

Alcohol

The attitude to alcohol and its availability varies between the different emirates. However, with the exception of Sharjah, it is generally served in licensed outlets that are associated with hotels (i.e. restaurants and bars), as well as a few health and sports clubs.

Shisha Pipes

Throughout the Middle East, smoking the traditional 'shisha' (water pipe), is a popular and relaxing pastime, usually savoured in a local café while chatting with friends.

The pipes can be smoked with a variety of aromatic flavours, such as strawberry or apple. This is one of the things in life that should be tried at least once!

Money

Cash is the preferred method of payment in the UAE, although credit cards are increasingly accepted. Cash and traveller's cheques can be exchanged in licensed exchange offices, banks and international hotels. There are no restrictions on the mport or export of any currency.

Local Currency

The monetary unit is the 'dirham' (Dhs.) which is divided into 100 'fils'. Notes come in denominations of Dhs.5, Dhs.10, Dhs.20, Dhs.50, Dhs.100, Dhs.200, Dhs.500 and Dhs.1,000. Coins are in denominations of 25, 50 and 100 fils or Dhs.1. The dirham has been tied to the US dollar since the end of 1980, at an approximate rate of US$ 1 = Dhs.3.67. Check the local press for the latest exchange rates.

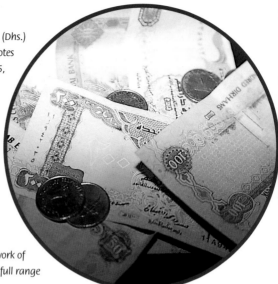

Banks

A well structured, and ever growing network of local and international banks offers the full range of banking services.

Hours: Saturday - Wednesday 08:00 - 13:00 (some also open 16:30 - 18:30); Thursday 08:00 - 12:00.

ATM's Most banks operate ATM's (Automatic Teller Machines, also known as cashpoints or service tills), which accept a wide range of cards.

Money Exchanges

Money exchanges can be found in all the main towns, offering good service and reasonable exchange rates. Exchange houses are open from 08:30 - 13:00 and 16:30 - 20:30.

Credit Cards

Most shops, hotels and restaurants accept the major credit cards (American Express, Diners Club, MasterCard, Visa). Smaller retailers are sometimes less keen to accept them and some may add an illegal 2 - 4% processing charge.

Tipping

Tipping practices are similar to most parts of the world. Service may be included in the bill, otherwise ten per cent is usual.

Add some depth to your lifestyle at
The Pavilion Dive Centre.

- Daily dive trips departing at 10 am. Trips to Musandam also available.
- Dive Dubai's favourite wreck sites.
- Full range of PADI dive courses available.
- Highly qualified PADI instructors.
- Enjoy the pleasant surroundings of The Jumeirah Beach Hotel.
- Retail centre - Mares dive equipment, Bodyglove wetsuits and a range of diving accessories.

Enriched Air Nitrox now available.

For more information and bookings call The Pavilion Dive Centre on 406-8827/28
Open 9 am - 6 pm daily

www.jumeirahinternational.com

Bargaining

Bargaining is a traditional part of doing trade in the UAE and it is still widely accepted, especially in the souks. It can be a fun and rewarding way to do business. Obviously, it's not always appropriate – so don't expect to bargain over your restaurant bill!

Entering the UAE

Visas

Visa requirements for entering the UAE vary and regulations should always be checked before travelling, as they are subject to change. The following nationals can now enter the UAE without obtaining a visa in advance. Their passports will be stamped with a Visit visa as they pass through Immigration on arrival. The countries are: Andorra, Australia, Austria, Bahrain, Belgium, Brunei, Canada, Cyprus, Denmark, Finland, Germany, Greece, Holland, Hong Kong, Iceland, Ireland, Italy, Japan, Kuwait, Liechtenstein, Luxembourg, Malaysia, Malta, Monaco, New Zealand, Norway, Oman, Portugal, Qatar, San Marino, Saudi Arabia, Singapore, Spain, Sweden, Switzerland, UK, USA and Vatican City. German and US citizens may obtain multiple entry visas from the UAE Embassies in their respective countries. Israeli nationals will not be issued visas.

Other citizens may obtain a visit visa from the UAE Embassy in their respective countries before departure. Alternatively a visa may be arranged through the sponsorship of a local UAE entity. This is commonly done by a local company such as a hotel, or by a local resident/business. The visa must be applied for before the visitor enters the country. Visitors may apply for an entry service permit (for 14 days), a visit visa (for 60 days, renewable) or a tourist visa (for 30 days, non-renewable).

Health Requirements

No health certificates are required, except for visitors who have been in a cholera or yellow fever infected area in the previous 14 days. However, it's always wise to check health recommendations before departure. Malarial mosquitoes are rare in the cities, although they do exist around the wadis and pools in the mountains.

Customs

It is forbidden to import drugs and pornographic items. All bags are x-rayed before you enter the country.

Duty free allowances: cigarettes – 2,000; cigars – 400; tobacco – 2 kg; alcohol (non-Muslim adults only) – 2 litres of spirits or 2 litres of wine; perfume – a reasonable amount.

Places to Stay

Visitors to the UAE will find an extensive and ever expanding choice of places to stay in Abu Dhabi and Dubai, from hotels to hotel apartments and even a youth hostel! Hotels range from those for visitors on a budget to world class outlets, offering superb facilities and service – there's something to suit every style and pocket! In the other emirates the choice of places to stay has increased over the last few years, but not to such an extent as in the two largest emirates. The larger hotels and hotel apartments will often act as a sponsor for those needing a visit visa. For hotel listings in the UAE please refer the next page.

For further information on where to stay in the UAE, refer to the **Dubai Explorer** and the **Abu Dhabi Explorer** guidebooks from Explorer Publishing. If you are considering a trip to Oman, the **Oman Explorer** guidebook covers everything you could ever want to know about this fascinating region of Arabia.

Getting Around

The car is the most popular method of getting around the UAE as a whole, either by private vehicle or taxi. There is also a growing public bus service. The road network is generally excellent and well signposted in Arabic and English.

Whilst the infrastructure is superb, the general standard of driving is not! Certain regulations have been introduced to make the roads safer, including a ban on using hand held mobile phones whilst driving and making it mandatory to wear seat belts in the front seats of a car. Speed limits are usually 60 - 80 km around town, while roads between cities are 100 - 120 km. If you are involved in a traffic accident, however minor, you must remain at the accident scene with your car and report the incident to the Traffic Police of that particular emirate.

Car Hire

All the main car rental companies, plus a few extra, are available and it's best to shop around as the rates and range of service vary. The rental company will usually arrange a temporary local driving license for visitors. Fully comprehensive insurance is a must.

Main Agents
Abu Dhabi Al Ghazal Transport Co (02 444 9300 / Al Ain 03 721 5222); Avis (02 632 3760 / 24 hour airport branch 02 575 7180 / Al Ain 03 768 7262); Budget (02 633 4200); Europcar (02 319 922); Fast Rent A Car (02 632 4000); Thrifty Car Rental (02 634 5663 / airport branch 02 575 7400).

UAE Hotels

Abu Dhabi (+971-2)

Al Dhafra Beach Hotel
Tel 877 1600   Fax 877 1354
Email **aafrant@emirates.net.ae**

Al Diar Gulf Hotel & Resort
Tel 441 4777   Fax 441 4537
Email **adglfhtl@emirates.net.ae**

Al Diar Sands Hotel
Tel 633 5335   Fax 633 5766
Email **sandshot@emirates.net.ae**

Corniche Residence Hilton
Tel 627 6000   Fax 627 0099
Email **corexflr@emirates.net.ae**

Crowne Plaza
Tel 621 0000   Fax 621 7444
Email **cpauh@emirates.net.ae**

Hilton Abu Dhabi
Tel 681 1900   Fax 681 1696
Email **auhhitw@emirates.net.ae**

Hilton Baynunah Tower
Tel 632 7777   Fax 621 6777
Email **baynunah@emirates.net.ae**

Hotel Inter-Continental Abu Dhabi
Tel 666 6888   Fax 666 9153
Email **abudhabi@interconti.com**

Khalidia Palace Hotel
Tel 666 2470   Fax 666 0411
Email **kphauh@emirates.net.ae**

Le Meridien Abu Dhabi
Tel 644 6666   Fax 644 0348
Email **meridien@emirates.net.ae**

Mafraq Hotel
Tel 582 2666   Fax 582 2899
Email **mafraq@emirates.net.ae**

Novotel Centre Hotel
Tel 633 3555   Fax 634 3633
Email **novoad@emirates.net.ae**

Zakher Hotel
Tel 627 5300   Fax 627 2270
Email **zakhotel@emirates.net.ae**

Ajman (+971-6)

Ajman Kempinski Hotel & Resort
Tel 745 1555   Fax 742 3336
Email **ajman.kempinski@kimp-aj.com**

Dubai (+971-4)

Hilton Dubai Jumeirah
Tel 399 1111   Fax 399 1112
Email **hiltonjb@emirates.net.ae**

Hotel Inter-Continental Dubai
Tel 222 7171   Fax 228 4777
Email **interconti_bc@iitrcdubai.co.ae**

Jumeirah Beach Club, The
Tel 344 5333   Fax 344 6222
Email **info@jumeirahbeachclub.com**

Jumeirah Beach Hotel
Tel 348 0000   Fax 348 2273
Email **jbh@jumeirah-beach.com**

Le Meridien Mina Seyahi
Tel 399 3333   Fax 399 3000
Email **reservations@lemeridien-minaseyahi.com**

Le Royal Meridien Beach Resort & Spa
Tel 399 5555   Fax 399 5999
Email **sales@leroyalmeridien.dubai.com**

Metropolitan Resort & Beach Club Hotel
Tel 399 5000   Fax 399 4547
Email **metbeach@emirates.net.ae**

Oasis Beach Hotel
Tel 399 4444   Fax 399 4200
Email **oasisbeachhotel@dutcohotels.com**

Ritz-Carlton Dubai
Tel 399 4000   Fax 399 4001
Email **rcdubai@emirates.net.ae**

Riviera Hotel
Tel 222 2131   Fax 221 1820
Email **riviera@emirates.net.ae**

Royal Mirage
Tel 399 9999   Fax 399 9998
Email **royalmirage@royalmiragedubai.com**

UAE Hotels

Sheraton Jumeirah Beach Resort & Towers
Tel **399 5533**   Fax **399 5577**
Email **sherjum@emirates.net.ae**

Fujairah (+971-9)

Al Diar Siji Hotel
Tel **223 2000**   Fax **223 2111**
Email **sijihotl@emirates.net.ae**

Fujairah Beach Motel
Tel **222 8111**   Fax **222 8054**
Email **fbm@emirates.net.ae**

Fujairah Hilton
Tel **222 2411**   Fax **222 6541**
Email **shjhiltwsal@hilton.com**

Holiday Beach Hotel
Tel **244 5540**   Fax **244 5580**
Email **holybemo@emirates.net.ae**

Ritz Plaza Hotel
Tel **224 1251**   Fax **222 2202**
Email **ritzplaza@emitates.net.ae**

Sandy Beach Motel
Tel **244 5555**   Fax **244 5200**
Email **sandybm@emirates.net.ae**

Hatta (+971-4)

Hatta Fort Hotel
Tel **852 3211**   Fax **852 3561**
Email **hfhhotel@emirates.net.ae**

Jazira (+971-2)

Al Diar Jazira Beach Resort & Hotel
Tel **562 9100**   Fax **562 9035**
Email **jazbeach@emirates.net.ae**

Jebel Ali (+971-4)

Jebel Ali Hotel & Golf Resort
Tel **883 6000**   Fax **883 5543**
Email **hoteluae@emirates.net.ae**

Khor Fakkan (+971-9)

Oceanic Hotel
Tel **238 5111**   Fax **238 7716**
Email **oceanic2@emirates.net.ae**

Ras Al Khaimah (+971-7)

Al Hamra Fort Hotel
Tel **244 6666**   Fax **244 6677**
Email **hamrafort@emirates.net.ae**

Dhafra Beach Hotel
Tel **872 3085**   Fax **877 1354**
Email – **n/a**

Ras Al Khaimah Hotel
Tel **236 2999**   Fax **236 2990**
Email **rakhotel@emirates.net.ae**

Sharjah (+971-6)

Holiday International
Tel **573 6666**   Fax **572 5060**
Email **holintsh@emirates.net.ae**

Marbella Resort
Tel **574 1111**   Fax **572 6050**
Email **maresort@emirates.net.ae**

Sharjah Continental Hotel
Tel **565 7777**   Fax **565 0090**
Email **shjconti@emirates.net.ae**

Sharjah Grand Hotel
Tel **528 5557**   Fax **528 2861**
Email **sales@sharjahgrand.com**

Umm Al Quwain (+971-6)

Barracuda Beach Resort
Tel **768 1555**   Fax **768 1556**
Email **baracuda@emirates.net.ae**

UAQ Tourist Club
Tel **765 0000**   Fax **765 0001**
Email **flaming1@emirates.net.ae**

Dubai Autolease (04 282 6565); Avis (04 224 5219); Budget (04 282 3030); Diamondlease Rent a Car (04 295 2111); Hertz Rent a Car (04 282 4422); Target Rent Car (04 272 0246); Thrifty Car Rental (04 337 0743); United Car Rentals (04 266 6286).
Sharjah Autobahn (06 536 0600); Autolease (06 573 5333); Budget (06 572 7600).

Taxis

If you don't have a car, taxis are the most common way of getting around. Each emirate has their own taxi firms, and charges are calculated either by meter or by agreeing the price before the journey.

Taxi Firms

Abu Dhabi Al Ghazal Taxis (02 444 7787).
Dubai Cars Taxis (white cars) (800 4825 / 04 269 3344); Dubai Transport Corporation (sand coloured cars) (04 208 0808); Gulf Radio Taxi (04 223 6666); National Taxis (silver cars) (04 336 6611);
Sharjah Delta Taxis (06 559 8598).

Media & Communications

Guidebooks

Numerous guidebooks exist on the UAE, from coffee table titles with glossy photographs to how to do business in this cosmopolitan environment. For a comprehensive breakdown of everything from where to stay, eat and drink to sports, shopping, culture and heritage, refer to the **Explorer Series** of guidebooks by Explorer Publishing. These include: **Abu Dhabi Explorer, Dubai Explorer, Kids Explorer, Off-Road Explorer**. While if you are including a trip to Oman in your visit to Arabia, check out the **Oman Explorer**.

Newspapers/Magazines

Gulf News, Khaleej Times and The Gulf Today (Dhs.2, Fridays Dhs.3), are the daily English language newspapers. Arabic newspapers include Al Bayan, Al Ittihad, Al Khaleej, Al Wahda and Al Fajr. Foreign newspapers and magazines are widely available from hotel bookshops and supermarkets.

Radio

The UAE has a number of commercial radio stations broadcasting in a range of languages, from Arabic and Hindi to English, French, Malayalam or Urdu. The English language stations are Ajman's Channel 4 FM (104.8Mhz FM), Dubai FM (92Mhz FM), Emirates FM1 (99.3 FM) and Emirates FM2 (98.7 FM). Frequencies and daily schedules can be found in the local newspapers.

Undiscovered Paradise
Unlimited Dive Adventure

Oman...The Essence of Arabia

Dimaniyat Islands Nature Reserve

Television / Satellite TV

Local television offers a number of Arabic and English language channels. The choice of what to watch is greatly increased by satellite TV, and most leading hotels and hotel apartments have stations available. These show everything from international entertainment or films to sports, cartoons and news programmes.

Post

Mail takes 6 - 10 days to reach Europe and the USA, 8 - 10 days to Australia and 5 - 10 days to India. Stamps can be bought from post offices, some card shops and supermarkets.

Red postal boxes for outbound mail are located at post offices and often near shopping centres. Your hotel will also handle post. For further information, check out the General Postal Authority website: www.gpa.gov.ae.

Telephones

The telephone network is run by Etisalat – the sole telecommunications provider in the UAE. Telephone calls within individual emirates are free of charge, except to or from mobile phones. Public payphones are found all over the place. Most require phonecards which are available from many shops and supermarkets.

Mobiles are extremely popular (the numbers are prefixed by 050), and the international GSM roaming service is available. If you do not have GSM for your phone, you may arrange for Etisalat's Speak Easy service, which will enable you to use your existing phone while in the UAE.

Internet

Etisalat is also responsible for Internet services within the UAE. Your hotel or hotel apartment may offer facilities for logging on, however, if you have your own computer you can use Etisalat's Dial 'n' Surf service. All that's needed is a computer with a modem and a regular phone or ISDN line. You then simply dial 500 5333 to gain access. Costs are billed to the phone line that is used. Call the help desk (800 5244) if you require further information.

Websites

There are numerous websites about the emirates, and new sites are continually being established.

http://dubaitourism.co.ae	Discover Dubai, business, news, online hotel reservations.
www.arabiaonline.com	Information and news on the Arab world.

www.dubai.com	Online newspaper type site.
www.dubaicityguide.com	Updated daily, lists upcoming events.
www.dubaionline.com	Information and news updated daily.
www.dubaishoppingmalls.com	List of shopping centres.
www.expatsite.com	Find out what's going on back home.
www.godubai.com	Covers all events and news in Dubai.
www.the-explorer.com	Comprehensive leisure and entertainment guide to Dubai.
www.UAEMall.com	Wide range of goods and services.

Medical Care

The quality of medical care varies considerably between the individual emirates. Visitors should have little trouble in getting treatment, whether privately or from the government hospitals in an emergency. Visitors are recommended to arrange medical insurance before travelling.

There are no specific health risks for visitors to face, although the climate can be harsh, especially during the summer months. It's advisable to drink plenty of water and to protect yourself from the sun.

Pharmacies/Chemists

Each emirate has at least one pharmacy open 24 hours. The location and telephone numbers are in the daily newspapers. In Dubai, an emergency Municipality number (04 223 2232), gives details of open chemists.

Insurance & Medical

As with any trip abroad, or potentially dangerous sport, it is important to arrange appropriate private medical insurance before leaving your home country. Private medical care in the UAE can be very expensive and a reasonable level of insurance cover with a respected company (while hopefully proving to be completely unnecessary), is well worthwhile.

Not all insurance companies will offer cover for sports diving, so check the small print. If you dive regularly you may find an annual insurance policy value for money (see if there is a limit on the number and length of trips). Remember to check how much, if any, excess you will have to pay in the event of a claim. Check also to see if there is any limit on the depth, number or type of dives you can make.

The basic elements that should be covered include the following:
- Cancellation.
- Missed or Delayed Departure.
- Loss of Personal Documents & Money.
- Loss of Personal Property (check if there's a limit on the value of single articles).
- Diving Equipment (this may not be required if you are hiring equipment check if there's a limit on the value of single articles).
- Personal Accident.
- Medical Cover (does this include emergency repatriation?).
- Hospital Benefit.
- Personal Liability.
- Legal Expenses & Assistance.
- Hyperbaric Treatment.

A specialist diving insurance company may be able to give advice on diving medicine and safety, offer first aid courses for divers or offer special deals for instructors. In particular, DAN Europe cover is designed specifically for divers.

DAN Europe
DAN Europe Headquarters PO Box DAN, 64026 Roseto, Italy
Tel **+39 (85) 893 0333**   Fax **+39 (85) 893 0050**   Email **mail@daneurope.org**
Website **www.daneurope.org**
Online membership application **esecur.htmesecur.htm**
Email **webmaster@daneurope.org**
Diving Emergencies **+41 (1) 383 1414**
DAN Travel Assist Non Diving Emergencies **+39 (39) 605 7858**

First Aid for Hazardous Marine Life

Hopefully you should never have any serious problems while out exploring, however, accidents DO happen! The following are some basic first aid pointers on how to cope with a close encounter with unpleasant marine life.

However, for the fuller picture refer to an approved first aid book. Bites and stings can be serious. The tricky part is often not knowing exactly what you have been stung or bitten by! When unsure, all bites/stings should be treated as serious and medical assistance sought.

For Emergency contact numbers please refer to page 178.

Definition of Icons

 Injury (Sting/Stab/Bite)

 Venom Toxic

 Secondary Infection

Hazardous Marine Life

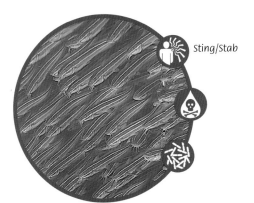

Sting/Stab

Catfish

- Control bleeding
- Immobilise limb
- Medical aid or hospitalisation may be required only rare fatalities have been recorded

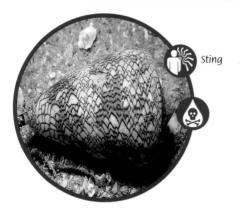

Cone Shell

Sting

- Pressure bandages, pain killers, CPR
- Wash wound with hot water (45-50°C), wound will have a milky appearance
- Immobilise limb
- In severe cases heart failure and death, Medical attention must be sought immediately

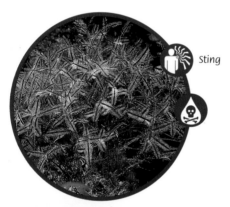

Hydroid Corals

Sting

- Apply vinegar or alcohol spirit for soothing
- Irritating and painful, not serious

Crown of Thorns Starfish

Sting

- Wash wound with hot water (45-50°C)
- Immobilise limb or lay victim down
- Remove spines/tentacles
- In serious cases the broken off venomous spines may require surgical removal

First Aid for Hazardous Marine Life

Jellyfish

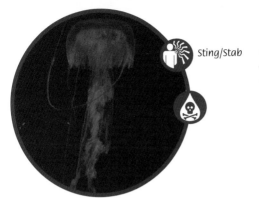

Sting/Stab

- Do not rub wound
- Remove tentacles
- Wash surface of the wound
- Apply ice pack followed by vinegar or alcohol spirit
- Most Jellyfish only cause irritation and pain, in rare cases severe stings have arrested breathing and caused heart failure

Lionfish

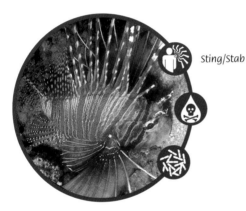

Sting/Stab

- Wash wound with hot water (45-50°C)
- Control bleeding
- Take pain killers to control pain
- Venom causes intense pain and difficulty in breathing, seek medical attention

Moray Eel

Bite

- Pressure bandages, painkillers and control bleeding
- Immobilise limb
- Serious secondary infections can result from being bitten, hospitalisation required

First Aid for Hazardous Marine Life

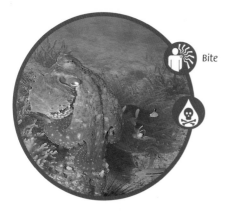

Octopus

Bite

- CPR, pressure bandages
- Milk wound
- Immobilise limb
- Keep limb lower than head and heart
- The venomous bite can cause fatal paralysis, medical attention must be sought immediately

Scorpion Fish

Sting/Stab

- Wash wound with hot water (45-50°C)
- Control bleeding, painkillers to control the pain
- Extreme pain and difficulty in breathing, seek medical attention

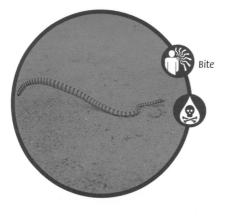

Sea Snake

Bite

- Milk wound
- CPR, pressure bandages
- Immobilise or lay victim down
- Keep limb lower than head and heart
- The venomous bite can cause fatal paralysis and cardiac arrest, medical attention must be sought immediately

Sea Urchin

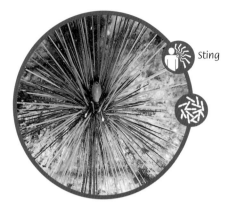

Sting

- Do not rub wound or remove spines or tentacles
- Wash surface of the wound with hot water (45-50°C)
- Apply vinegar or alcohol spirit
- In most cases the body dissolves the spines but in rare instances they may need surgical removal

Stonefish

Sting/Stab

- Milk wound
- Immobilise limb
- CPR, pressure bandages
- Painkillers, immobilised/laydown
- The sting can cause fatal paralysis and cardiac arrest, medical attention must be sought immediately

Toxopneustes

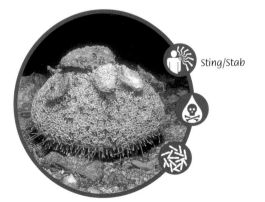

Sting/Stab

- Wash wound with hot water (45-50°C)
- Immobilise limb or lay victim down
- Remove spines
- Medical attention must be sought immediately

Environment & the Law

After years of neglect, the UAE is finally taking steps to protect its environment. Federal Law No. 23 issued by the UAE President, HH Sheikh Zayed bin Sultan Al Nahyan provides for the use, protection and development of water resources. The law includes a set of rules to regulate fishing and navigation activities in UAE waters, which are designed to protect the marine life and water resources. The law came into being following concern raised by experts over the depletion of fisheries in UAE waters.

Over the past few years, lack of care by some fishermen using illegal fishing equipment has resulted in extensive harm to marine life and coral. Nylon nets, for example, yield a larger catch of fish, but also trap and harm other marine life. In addition to such malpractice is the pollution caused by fishing and transportation vessels. These factors have reduced fish stocks in the region. In accordance with the law, commercial fishermen need a license from the Ministry of Agriculture and Fisheries to be able to fish. Violators are prosecuted and penalties include fines and possible imprisonment. All equipment belonging to violators is impounded.

The Federal Law for Environmental Development and Protection deals with issues affecting the development of the environment. It includes a wide range of protection for the marine environment. For instance, on the East Coast certain sites have been established as special marine reserves. However, although there are boards displayed on the shore to indicate these reserves, the rules appear to be ignored by some fishermen, (perhaps due to lack of enforcement or awareness?).

Sharjah's ruler bans fishing of sea turtles. Details are found under the dive site Jazirat Sir Bu Na'air.

The seas around us have taken thousands of years to evolve, but are gradually being destroyed. UAE marine life is priceless, and on a more personal level, we would like to encourage you to actively help protect it, by complying with the following:
- Do not remove any creatures (even if they appear to be dead).
- Do not 'ride' turtles; they will panic and drown.
- Do not throw rubbish into the water.
- Do not touch ANY marine creature; you will be able to watch them longer if you do not disturb them.

F A S T
First Aid & Safety Training
C O N S U L T A N T S

FIRST AID

A range of first aid courses conducted by St John Ambulance licensed trainers to international standards. Community or corporate courses to your requirements, or attend our programme of open courses at the Dubai Tennis Stadium.

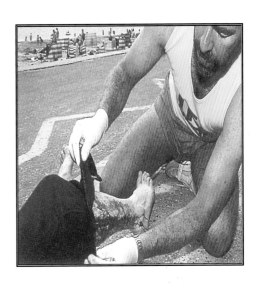

COMMUNITY HEALTH & SAFETY

If it is safety related, we can help. Courses are available in subjects as diverse as fire awareness / food hygiene / personal security / pool safety / lifesaving / defensive and off-road driving. Whether it is training for your nanny / maid, a group activity or to improve your own skills and knowledge, we have a course for you.

OUR TRAINING POLICY

"We believe that training should equip the candidates to DO the skills and procedures in REAL places, and not just pass an exam or recite theory. Our courses give as much hands on experience as possible, encouraging trainees to work things out for themselves, and we provide realism wherever possible.

We understand that someone's LIFE or SAFETY could depend upon this".

INDUSTRIAL COURSES

The UAE is very quickly catching up with the world's established capitals, and occupational health and safety is becoming increasingly relevant. Health & Safety Awareness and Management / COSHH / Fire / Manual Handling / Risk Assessment / PPE / H&S in Construction / Forklift Trucks. Whatever your problem, we will have the solution.

Working for Industry and the Community

Licensed Trainer

Member

Member

PO Box 27056 - Dubai - UAE (Tel) 04-2826470 (Fax) 04-2865125
Email – fastsvcs@emirates.net.ae

- Do not touch corals; hard corals are made up of millions of zooxanthellae which they need for growth and to form the foundation of their limestone skeleton. Soft corals consist of delicate polyps, usually in eight-polyp segments, known as octocorals. By touching them, you kill them. Note that coral cuts are infectious and take a long time to heal.
- Collect rubbish; plastic bags, old bottles, discarded nets, etc. (after checking for any hidden creatures to ensure that they are empty).
- Maintain buoyancy.
- Take care when anchoring.
- If you have a picnic, either use the trash bins provided on the beaches, or take the rubbish away with you.

Emirates Diving Association (EDA)

EDA was initiated in 1995 by instruction of HH Sheikh Zayed Bin Sultan Al Nahyan, President of the UAE, who recognized the importance of diving and the need to protect UAE marine life.

EDA promote sustainable development of marine natural resources in UAE, and their mission statement is "to conserve, protect and restore the UAE marine resources by understanding and promoting the marine environment".

Emirates Environmental Group (EEG)

EEG started during the early 1990's with a core team of six ladies who recognized that much needed to be done to maintain the beauty and cleanliness of Dubai. Using their homes and various offices to conduct business and meetings (including UAE municipality offices) until an office was donated to them by Mohammad Abdul Jalil Al Fahim in 1997. EEG is still represented by one of those founding members, Ms Habiba Al-Marashi.

The aims and objectives of Emirates Environmental Group is to provide the general public and businesses alike with information on the status of recycling facilities and recyclable items available in Dubai, thus encouraging all to participate actively in establishing schemes.

To find out about EEG view their website: www.eeg-uae.com

UAE Dive Directory

Abu Dhabi (+971-2)

Abu Dhabi Sub Aqua Club
Al Meena Zayed
Tel **673 1111**   Fax **673 1113**
Email **theclub@emirates.net.ae**

Abu Dhabi Tourist Club
Near Le Meridien Hotel
Tel **672 3400**   Fax **677 2516**
Email **adclub@emirates.net.ae**

Blue Dolphin Company LLC
Hotel Inter-Continental Abu Dhabi
Tel **666 9392**   Fax **666 6802**
Email **sindbadbd@hotmail.com**

Golden Boats
Le Meridien Abu Dhabi
Tel **665 9929**   Fax **667 3735**
Email **goldmat@emirates.net.ae**

Ajman (+971-6)

Ajman Kempinski Hotel & Resort
Tel **745 1555**   Fax **745 1222**
Email **ajman.kempinski@kempaj.com**

Dubai (+971-4)

Al Boom Diving
Al Wasl Road
Tel **342 2993**   Fax **342 2995**
Email **abdiving@emirates.net.ae**

Club Mina
Le Meridien Mina Seyahi
Tel **399 3333**   Fax **399 3111**
Email **dimccomm@emirates.net.ae**

Emirates Diving Association
Tel **393 9390**   Fax **393 9391**
Email **edadiver@emirates.net.ae**

Inner Space Diving Centre
Heritage & Diving Village
Tel **393 7775**   Fax **393 7774**
Email **innerspc@emirates.net.ae**

Oasis Beach Club
Oasis Beach Hotel
Tel **399 4444**   Fax **399 4200**
Email
oasisbeachhotel@dutcohotels.com

Pavilion Dive Centre
Jumeirah Beach Hotel
Tel **406 8827**   Fax **348 4754**
Email **phil.oshea@jumeirahbeach
hotel.com**

Scuba Dubai
Trade Centre Apartments
Tel **331 7433**   Fax **331 0680**
Email **info@scubadubai.com**

Scubatec
Sana Building
Tel **334 8988**   Fax **336 6461**
Email **scubatec@emirates.net.ae**

Fujairah (+971-9)

Charlotte Anne Charters
Fujairah International Marina
Tel **222 3508**   Fax **222 3508**
Email **seatrips@emirates.net.ae**

Sandy Beach Diving Centre
Sandy Beach Motel
Tel **244 5050**   Fax **244 5900**
Email **sbdiving@emirates.net.ae**

Scuba 2000
Al Badiya Beach
Tel **050 649 5540**   Fax **554 0413**
Email dim@emirates.net.ae

Scuba International
Heritage & Diving Village
Tel **393 7557**   Fax **393 7883**
Email **scubaint@emirates.net.ae**

Khor Fakkan (+971-9)

**Al Madhani Sea Tourist & Diving
Near Dibba Oman**
Tel **0506905080** Fax **2383370**

UAE & Oman Dive Directory

Diving House
On the corniche road
Tel **238 3638**   Fax   **238 7383**
Email   **dive4fun@emirates.net.ae**

Divers Down
Tel **237 0299**   Fax **237 0194**
Email   **diversdown@emirates.net.ae**

Ocean Divers Centre
Oceanic Hotel
Tel **238 2971**   Fax **238 2971**
Email   **scubaint@emirates.net.ae**

Seven Seas Diving Centre
Near Khor Fakkan Souk
Tel **238 7400**   Fax **238 7440**
Email   **diving@emirates.net.ae**

Sharjah (+971-6)

Sharjah Dive Club
Sharjah Wanderers Sports Club
Tel **535 7505**   Fax **535 3826**
Email **joescott@emirates.net.ae**

Oman

Barka (+968)

Ocean Extreme Dive Centre
Al Sawadi Resort
Tel **895 545**   Fax **895 535**
Email **forumalsawadi@interconti.com**

Khasab (+968)

Khasab Travel & Tours
Tel **830 464**   Fax **830 364**
Dubai Tel (+971) 4 266 9950
Email **khastour@omantel.net.om**

Marbella (+968)

Al Ghadeer Tours
Tel **932 5441**   Fax **894 040**
Email **riyathgm@omancel.net.om**

Muscat (+968)

Blu Zone Diving
Marina Bander Al-Rowdha
Tel **737 293**   Fax **737 293**
Email **bluzone@gto.net.om**

Diveco
Tel **602 101**   Fax **602542**
Email **diveco@omantel.net.om**

Muscat Divers
Marina Bander Al-Rowdha
Tel **618 047**   Fax **502 230**
Email **marina@omancel.net.om**

Oman Discovery
Tel **706 424**   Fax **7060463**
Email **omandisc@omalcel.net.om**

Oman Dive Centre
Bandar Jassah
Tel **950 261**   Fax **799 600**
Email **diveoman@omancel.net.om**
Website: **www.diveoman.com.om**

Qurum Beach Hotel
Tel **564 070**   Fax **560 761**
Email **qurumbeaachhotel@hotmail.com**

Sera Divers
Tel **611 314**   Fax **611 314**
Email **martyn@gto.net.om**

Sunny Day Water Sports
Al Bustan Palace Hotel
Tel **700 712**   Fax **700 812**
Email **albustan@interconti.com**

Dive Site Co-ordinates

West Coast

Dive Site	Lat/Long in DMS (WGS 84)	Distance, Headings (Reciprocal)
Anchor Barge	N 25° 30' 48" (.850') E 55° 04' 36" (.633')	Dubai Creek 18.6nm @ 319° (139°) DOSC 21.5nm @ 336° (156°) Mina Seyahi 25.4nm @ 350° (170°)
Barge 58	N 25° 20' 06" (.093') E 55° 03' 17" (.289')	DOSC 13nm @ 316° (136°) Dubai Creek 13.5nm @ 284° (104°) Mina Seyahi 15.2nm @ 340° (160°)
Barracuda Barge	N 25° 27' 16" (.260') E 55° 22' 41" (.690')	DOSC 18.8m @ 026° (206°) Dubai Creek 11.5nm @ 024° (204°) Mina Seyahi 25.1nm @ 030° (210°)
Car Barge & Tug	N 25° 16' 16" (.270') E 55° 08' 02" (.048')	Dubai Creek 8.8nm @ 268° (88°) DOSC 7.4nm @ 321° (141°) Mina Seyahi 10.7nm @ 356° (176°)
Cement Barge (Alamina)	N 25° 10' 20" (.333') E 55° 12' 17" (.283')	Dubai Creek 7.8nm @ 217° (37°) DOSC 0.7nm @ 257° (77°) Mina Seyahi 5.7nm @ 034° (214°)
MV Dara	N 25° 34' 29" (.484') E 55° 27' 58" (.977')	Dubai Creek 20.3nm @ 025° (205°) DOSC 27.4nm @ 28° (208°) Hamriya 6.2nm @ 339° (159°)
DB1/SMB	N 25° 16' 48" (.800') E 55° 03' 43" (.716')	Dubai Creek 12.6nm @ 270° (90°) DOSC 10.5nm @ 306° (126°) Mina Seyahi 12nm @ 337° (157°)
Energy Determination	N 26° 04' 08" (.133') E 55° 34' 04" (.068')	Dubai Creek 49.9nm @ 016° (196°) DOSC 56.7nm @ 018° (198°) Hamriya 35nm @ 004° (184°)
Hammour Barge	N 25° 04' 40" (.675') E 54° 46' 06" (.108')	DOSC 25.1nm @ 255° (075°) Jebel Ali Marina 14.9nm @ 290° (110°) Mina Seyahi 20.4nm @ 266° (086°)
Hannan	N 24° 50' 11" (.183') E 53° 53' 34" (.566')	Jebel Ali Marina 62.5nm @ 290° (260°) The Club Abu Dhabi 33.3nm @ 304° (124°)
Hopper Barge (HB6)	N 25° 30' 28" (.465') E 55° 03' 59" (.976')	Dubai Creek 18.7nm @ 317° (137°) DOSC 21.5nm @ 336° (156°) Mina Seyahi 25.1nm @ 349° (169°) Neptune to Hopper Barge 0.18nm @ 223° (43°)

Dive Site Co-ordinates

Dive Site	Lat/Long in DMS	Distance, Headings (Reciprocal)
Jaramac III	N 25° 16' 43" (.766') E 55° 03' 36" (.616')	DB1 75m @ 81° (261°) Dubai Creek 12.7nm @ 270° (90°) DOSC 10.6nm @ 305° (125°) Mina Seyahi 12nm @ 336° (156°)
Jaramac V	N 25° 16' 49" (.818') E 55° 03' 47"(.782')	DB1 0.1nm @ 251° (71°) Dubai Creek 12.7nm @ 270° (90°) DOSC 10.4nm @ 305° (125°) Mina Seyahi 12nm @ 337° (157°)
Jasim	N 24° 58' 50" (.816') E 54° 29' 45" (.716')	Dubai Creek 46.9nm @ 246° (66°) Jebel Ali Marina 28.9 nm @ 268° (88°) Mina Seyahi 36nm @ 258° (78°)
Jazirat Sir Bu Na'air	N 25° 13' 30" (.500') E 54° 13' 00" (.000')	Dubai Creek 58.7nm @ 266° (86°) Jebel Ali Marina 46.3nm @ 286° (106°) Mina Seyahi 51.1nm @ 278° (98°)
Jebel Ali Ferry	N 25° 05' 12" (.200') E 54° 52' 24" (.400')	Dubai Creek 25.5nm @ 242° (62°) DOSC 19.4nm @ 252° (72°) Jebel Ali Marina 10.2nm @ 304° (124°) Mina Seyahi 14.7nm @ 267° (87°)
Jumeirah Artificial Reef	N 25° 09' 37" (.608') E 55° 09' 30" (.549')	Dubai Creek 9.9nm @ 266° (86°) DOSC 3.3nm @ 253° (73°) Mina Seyahi 4.1nm @ 010° (190°)
Lion City	N 25° 00' 13" (.224') E 54° 31' 44" (.733')	DOSC 38.8nm @ 253° (73°) Jebel Ali Marina 27nm @ 270° (90°) Mina Seyahi 33.9nm @ 259° (79°)
MV Ludwig	N 25° 06' 54" (.895') E 54° 34' 14" (.231')	DOSC 35.3nm @ 262° (82°) Jebel Ali Marina 25.9nm @ 286° (106°) Mina Seyahi 31.2nm @ 271° (91°)
Nasteran	N 25° 28' 00" (.000') E 55° 21' 22" (.367')	Dubai Creek 12nm @ 0.15° (195°) DOSC 18.9nm @ 022° (202°) Hamriya Creek 7.4nm @ 262° (82°) Mina Seyahi 25.2nm @ 028° (208°)
Neptune	N 25° 30' 20"(.333') E 55° 03' 50"(.833')	Dubai Creek 18.7nm @ 317° (137°) DOSC 21.5nm @ 336 (156°) Mina Seyahi 25nm @ 349° (169°)

Dive Site Co-ordinates

Dive Site	Lat/Long in DMS	Distance, Headings (Reciprocal)
Old Cement Barge, Abu Dhabi	N 24° 32' 56" (.929') E 54° 19' 36" (.604')	-
Pipeline Barge	N 25° 31' 30" (.500') E 55° 08' 46" (.766')	Dubai Creek 17.1nm @ 330° (155°) DOSC 21.3nm @ 348° (168°)
Rashid Wrecks (North of Breakwater)	N 25° 16' 51" (.860') E 55° 15' 54" (.900')	Dubai Creek 1.6nm @ 285° (105°) DOSC 6.8nm @ 022° (202°) Mina Seyahi 13nm @ 029° (209°)
Rashid Wrecks (South of Breakwater)	N 25° 15' 45" (.750') E 55° 15' 23" (.390')	Dubai Creek 2.1nm @ 251° (71°) DOSC 5.6nm @ 022° (202°) Mina Seyahi 11.9nm @ 030° (210°)
MV Sarraf Three	N 25° 16' 07" (.114') E 55° 07' 55" (.920')	DB1 3.9nm @ 279° (99°) Dubai Creek 8.8nm @ 267° (87°) DOSC 7.3nm @ 319° (139°) Mina Seyahi 10.5nm @ 355° (175°)
Zainab	N 25° 14' 93" (.236') E 54° 51' 54" (.900')	Dubai Creek 23.8nm @ 265° (85°) DOSC 20nm @ 281° (101°) Mina Seyahi 18.1nm @ 300° (120°)

Musandam

Dive Site	Lat/Long in DMS	Distance, Headings (Reciprocal)
Bu Rashid	N 26° 24' 12" (.200') E 56° 29' 42"(.700')	Dibba Bayah 46.6nm @ 015°
Caves, The	N 25° 48' 14" (.240') E 56° 22' 03"(.050')	Dibba Bayah 10.6nm @ 028°(208°)
Ennerdale Rock	N 26° 27' 40" (.659') E 56° 22' 03"(.953')	Dibba Bayah 50.2nm @ 015°
Fanaku Island	N 26° 29' 55" (.918') E 56° 31' 50"(.840')	Dibba Bayah 52.5nm @ 016°
Great Quion Island	N 26° 30' 21" (.349') E 56° 30' 52"(.860')	Dibba Bayah 52.8nm @ 014°
Hard Rock Cafe Ras Bashin	N 26° 12' 13" (.217') E 56° 29' 18"(.308')	Dibba Bayah 35nm @ 020°

Dive Site	Lat/Long in DMS	Distance, Headings (Reciprocal)
Hamra	N 25° 55' 21" (.345') E 56° 26' 39" (.645')	Dibba Bayah 18.8nm @ 028° (208°)
Jazirat Al Khayl	N 26° 22' 24" (.400') E 56° 26' 51" (.850')	Dibba Bayah 44.2nm @ 012°
Jazirat Hamra	N 26° 16' 54" (.900') E 56° 27' 12" (.200')	Dibba Bayah 38.9nm @ 015°
		Dibba Bayah 45.4nm @ 019°
Jazirat Musandam	N 26° 22' 11" (.190') E 56° 32' 18" (.300')	
		Dibba Bayah 39.7nm @ 014°
Jazirat Sawda	N 26° 17' 43" (.710') E 56° 27' 12" (.200')	
		Dibba Bayah 35nm @ 025°
Jazirat Sawda	N 26° 10' 32" (.532') E 56° 32' 47" (.787')	
		Dibba Bayah 46.8nm @ 018°
Kachalu Island	N 26° 23' 46" (.759') E 56° 31' 48" (.801')	Dibba Bayah 20.3nm @ 029° (209°)
Lima Rock	N 25° 56' 27" (.453') E 56° 27' 51" (.853')	Dibba Bayah 31nm @ 022°
Ras Dillah	N 26° 07' 51" (.850') E 56° 29' 16" (.270')	Dibba Bayah 31.6nm @ 021°
Ras Dillah Ghubbat Ash Shabus Bay	N 26° 08' 37" (.622') E 56° 28' 47" (.786')	Dibba Bayah 36.8nm @ 019°
Ras Khaysay	N 26° 14' 00" (.000') E 56° 29' 24" (.400')	Dibba Bayah 20.4nm @ 028° (208°)
Ras Lima	N 25° 56' 46" (.680') E 56° 27' 31" (.580')	Dibba Bayah 46.2nm @ 017°
Ras Musandam	N 26° 23' 12" (.202') E 56° 31' 29" (.485')	Dibba Bayah 41.6nm @ 018°
Ras Qabr Al Hindi	N 26° 18' 34" (.563') E 56° 30' 52" (.869')	

Dive Site Co-ordinates

Dive Site	Lat/Long in DMS	Distance, Headings (Reciprocal)
Ras Sarkan	N 26° 04' 36" (.604') E 56° 28' 55" (.910')	Dibba Bayah 27.9nm @ 024°
Ruqq Suwayk	N 26° 24' 12" (.199') E 56° 28' 42" (.702')	Dibba Bayah 46.5nm @ 014°
Pearl Island	N 25° 57' 37" (.610') E 56° 25' 52" (.864')	Dibba Bayah 20.6nm @ 031° (211°)
Octopus Rock	N 26° 00' 02" (.020') E 56° 26' 20" (.340')	Dibba Bayah 23nm @ 022° (202°)
Ras Marovi	N 25° 59' 06" (.094') E 56° 26' 09" (.145')	Dibba Bayah 21nm @ 024° (204°)
White Rock, Ras Khaysay	N 26° 14' 14" (.236') E 56° 29' 43" (.716')	Dibba Bayah 37.1nm @ 019°
Ras Marovi	N 25° 59' 06" (.094') E 56° 26' 09" (.145')	Dibba Bayah 21nm @ 024° (204°)

East Coast

Dive Site	Lat/Long in DMS	Distance, Headings (Reciprocal)
Anemone Gardens	N 25° 21' 01" (.020') E 56° 22' 47" (.780')	Khor Fakkan Harbour 1nm @ 081° (261°) Lulaya Harbour 2.1nm @ 179° (359°)
Car Cemetery	N 25° 25' 07" (.117') E 56° 22' 34" (.570')	Khor Fakkan Harbour 4nm @ 081° (261°) Lulaya Harbour 1.6nm @ 350° (170°)
Coral Gardens	N 25° 21' 12"(.200') E 56° 22' 48"(.800')	Khor Fakkan Harbour 1nm @ 081° (261°) Lulaya Harbour 2.1nm @ 179° (359°)
Dibba Island	N 25° 36' 06" (.100') E 56° 20' 05"(.080')	Khor Fakkan Harbour 15.2nm @ 353° (173°) Lulaya Harbour 12.8nm @ 347° (167°)
Inchcape 1	N 25° 30' 45" (.750') E 56° 22' 57"(.950')	Khor Fakkan Harbour 10nm @ 130° (193°) Lulaya Harbour 7nm @ 015° (195°)
Inchcape 2	N 25° 20' 20" (.576') E 56° 22' 53"(.823')	Khor Fakkan Harbour 15.2nm @ 353° (173°) Lulaya Harbour 3.14nm @ 167° (347°)
Forbidden Beach	N 25° 31' 18" (.300') E 56° 22' 12" (.200')	Khor Fakkan Harbour 10.2nm @ 537° (173°)
Martini Rock	N 25° 20' 05"(.086') E 56° 22' 53" (.884')	Khor Fakkan Harbour 1.3nm @122° (302°) Lulaya Harbour 3.3nm @ 179°(359°)

Dive Site Co-ordinates

Dive Site	Lat/Long in DMS	Distance & Headings (Reciprocal)
Ras Qidfa	N 25° 19' 27"(.452') E 56° 22' 56"(.932')	Khor Fakkan Harbour 2.1nm @ 204° (024°) Lulaya Harbour 4.9nm @ 201° (021°)
Shark Island (Khor Fakkan Island)	N 25° 21' 12"(.200') E 56° 22' 36" (.600')	Khor Fakkan Harbour 1nm @ 081°(261°) Lulaya Harbour 2.4nm @ 183° (003°)
Sharm Rocks (Rock Piles/ Three Rocks)	N 25° 28' 55"(.917') E 56° 21' 57" (.952')	Khor Fakkan Harbour 8.7nm @ 353°(173°) Lulaya Harbour 5.2nm @ 348° (168°)
Snoopy Island (Jazirat Al Ghubbah)	N 25° 29' 29" (.480') E 56° 21' 59" (.922')	Khor Fakkan Harbour 8nm @ 359° (179°) Lulaya Harbour 5.5nm @ 350° (170°)

Glossary

Aft	The area towards the stern of the boat.
Beam	The greatest width of the boat.
Bow	The area towards the front of the boat.
Bridge	The location from which a vessel is steered and its speed controlled.
Bulkhead	A vertical partition separating compartments.
Buoy	An anchored float used for marking a mooring or position in the water.
Deck	A permanent covering over a compartment, hull or any part thereof.
Draft	The depth of water a boat draws.
DWT	Dead-weight (see explanation under Diving the West Coast).
GPS	Global positioning system (satellite navigation system).
Hatch	An opening in a boat's deck, fitted with a watertight cover.
Hold	A compartment below deck in a large vessel, used solely for carrying cargo.
Hull	The main body of a vessel.
LC	Landing craft.
MV	Motor vessel.
Nautical mile	One minute of latitude; approximately 6076 feet – about 1/8 longer than a statute mile of 5280 feet or 1852 metres.
Neap Tides	The least tidal movement. These occure twice a month when the moon is at right angles to the sun; this happens on the moon's first and third quarters. When the combined gravitational pull of both the moon and the sun is the weakest this creates the lowest high waters and the highest low waters tides.
Port	The left side of a boat with bow in front (red light).
Reciprocal	After travelling from A to B, the opposite bearing to return from B to A.
Screw	The boat's propeller.
Spring Tides	The greatest tidal movement. These occur twice a month when the moon and the sun are in line; this happens on new and full moons. When the combined gravitational pull of both the moon and the sun is the strongest this creates the highest high waters and the lowest low waters tides.
Starboard	The right side of a boat with bow in front (green light).
Stern	The back area of the boat.
Thermoclines	A layer of colder water sandwiched between the warmer well-mixed surface water layer and the colder denser lower layer. Seasonal thermoclines form layers in the shallower depths.
VLCC	Very large crude carrier.

References

Lloyd's List

Prior to 1741, there was no centralised information source on shipwrecks. Instead, details were kept locally, although information on a limited number of incidents was traceable through secondary sources, such as a checklist of narratives of shipwrecks and disasters at sea. From 1741, the date of the first surviving issue, the Lloyd's List provided a daily record of information on shipping casualties. As the intelligence network of Lloyd's of London grew, this source became increasingly comprehensive, covering not only British vessels and vessels wrecked in British waters, but shipping losses worldwide.

A variety of indexes is available from the Guildhall Library (Aldermanbury, London EC2P 2EJ, UK). Both this and other records of losses compiled by Lloyd's of London are described at length in the second edition of the Guide to the Lloyd's Marine Collection by Declan Barriskill (London: Guildhall Library, 1994).

From 1856 onwards, reports of inquiries were also published in newspapers, most notably Mitchell's Maritime Register, 1856-1884, and the Shipping Gazette (Lloyd's List Weekly Summary).

Lloyd's Register & the Mercantile Navy List

'Posted' editions of the Lloyd's Register of Ships often indicates the fate of a vessel, the entry being stamped 'collision', 'foundered', 'condemned' etc., sometimes with the month and year added (3.89). The month and year refer to the relevant quarter of the Lloyd's Register Casualty Return, published from 1890 to date. The Lloyd's Register Casualty Returns are available for research at Lloyd's Register (100, Leadenhall Street, London, EC3A 3BP, UK).

The Mercantile Navy List is never posted but, from 1875-1904, lists of vessels removed from the British register while the current issue was going to press are included, with brief reasons why. Separate monthly returns, listing vessels added or removed, were also printed. The Public Records Office (Ruskin Avenue, Kew, Richmond, Surrey TW9 4DU, UK), has bound volumes of these for the period 1875-1890; and the Guildhall Library has them for 1890-1946. These are particularly useful for vessels not actually lost at sea, but hulked, laid up or condemned as unseaworthy.

Bibliography

Shipwrecks – Useful Books
• Dictionary of Disasters at Sea During the Age of Steam, by Charles Hocking (London: Lloyd's Register of Shipping, 1969)

• Modern Shipping Disasters 1963-1987 by Norman Hooke (London: Lloyd's of London Press, 1989)

Shipwrecks – Other Sources of Information
• Wreck Section, Hydrographic Department, Ministry of Defence, Taunton, Somerset TA12 2DN   United Kingdom

Provides an information service for commercial, private, Ministry of Defence and other government department enquiries. Has information on all post 1913 marine casualties occurring in continental shelf areas, except for American and Australian coastal waters. A search fee is charged.

• Lloyd's Marine Collection, Guildhall Library, Aldermanbury, London EC2P 2EJ United Kingdom

Information on marine casualties and shipping movements worldwide from about 1740. Sources include Lloyd's List, war loss records, etc. Open to the public.

• Information Group, Lloyd's Register of Shipping, 100 Leadenhall Street, London EC3A 3BP United Kingdom

Brief ship details, date and place of losses recorded in the quarterly returns, post 1890. This small specialist library includes some books on shipwrecks. Open to the public.

MV Dara Disaster
• Last hours of the Dara by PJ Abraham
• The Grey-Widow Maker by Bernard Edward
• Khaleej Times magazine April 4, 1980 by Ian Bain

Bibliography

Other more general reference books and guidebooks are numerous.   The following list includes our favourites, and those most appropriate for UAE waters.

Marine Life
• Coral Reef Animals of the Indo-Pacific by Terrence M. Gosliner, David W. Behrens & Gary C. Williams (order from Sea Challengers, California, USA)
• The Coral Seas of Muscat by Frances Green & Richard Keech (ISBN 0-946510-28-8)
• Indo-Pacific Coral Reef Field Guide by Dr Gerald R. Allen & Roger Steene (ISBN 981-00-5687-7)
• Nudibranchs & Sea Snails by Helmut Debelius (order from IKAN, Germany)
 • Seashells of Oman by Donald & Eloise Bosch (ISBN 0-582-78309-7)
  • Indian Ocean Reef Guide by Helmut Debelius (order from IKAN, Germany) Also sold by Scuba Dubai

First Aid & Safety
  • The Diving Emergency Handbook by John Lippmann & Stan Bugg (ISBN 0-946-02018-3)
   • A Medical Guide to Hazardous Marine Life by Paul S. Auerbach (Best Publishing, January 1999 paperback) (ISBN 0-941-33255-1)
    • Red Sea Safety - Guide to Dangerous Marine Animals by Dr Peter Vine (Immel Publishing) (ISBN 0-907-15112-4)

Acknowledgements

We would like to acknowledge the following people and companies for their assistance, providing inspiration, time, interest, information and knowledge, without whom we would not have been able to write this book.

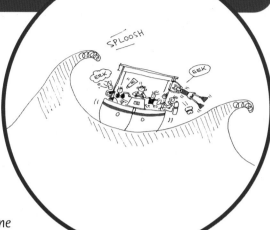

Dive Buddies & Explorers
Ali Fikree, Andrew Smith, Christine Schroder, Guy Ploegaerts, John Tilley, Leon Betts and Phil Holt

Photographs, sketches and cartoons
Special Thanks to:
- John Gregory for his help with the ships' weights and measures and the drawing of the *Neptune*
- Leon Betts for his drawings of the *Car Cemetery*, *Dibba Island*, *Martini Rock* and *Sharm Rocks*.
- Geoff Taylor for the drawing of the *Dara*.
- Brian Davies for the photographs of the *Energy Determination* and *Dara*.
- Andrew Bingham Smith for the cartoons.
- Terry Day for the photographs of the *Energy Determination*.

Companies
- Stephanie Davies at Scuba Dubai
- Louise Denly and Karen Hibbs at J. Ray McDermott
- Seraj Alali at White Sea Shipping
- Maps geosystems for the satellite images
- Eric Laing and Capt. Joe Finch at Inchcape Shipping Services

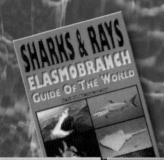

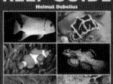
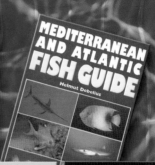
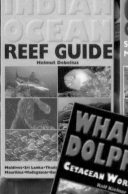

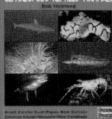

Harbour Maps & Co-ordinates

West Coast

The Club Slipway
Abu Dhabi

N 24° 30' 46"
E 54° 23' 18"

Public Slipway
Abu Dhabi

N 29° 30' 45"
E 54° 22' 26"

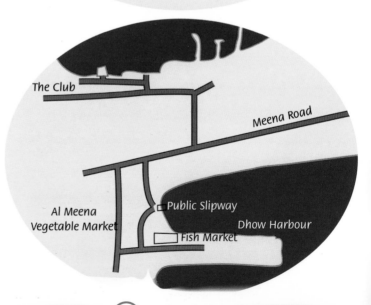

Jebel Ali Hotel Marina
Jebel Ali

N 24° 59' 16"
E 55° 01' 32"

Hotel

Marina slipway
a fee of Dhs50 per boat
is charged at the
security gate

Golf Course

Dubai - Abu Dhabi Road (old road)

Jebel Ali
Shooting Club

To the port

Take exit 13 on Sheikh Zayed Road

To Dubai

Dubai Creek Mouth
Dubai

N 25° 16' 44"
E 55° 17' 36"

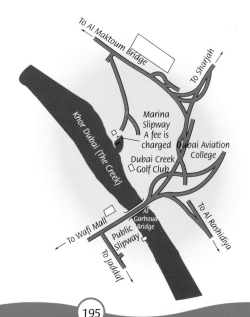

To Al Maktoum Bridge

To Sharjah

Khor Dubai (The Creek)

Marina
Slipway
A fee is
charged

Dubai Aviation
College

Dubai Creek
Golf Club

To Al Rashidiya

To Wafi Mall

Al
Garhoud
Bridge

Public
Slipway

To Jaddaf

Dubai International Marine Club (DIMC)
Dubai

N 25° 05' 32"
E 55° 08' 34"

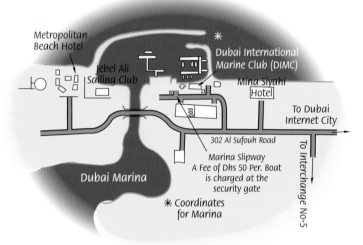

Dubai Offshore Sailing Club (DOSC) Harbour
Dubai

N 25° 10' 37"
E 55° 12' 56"

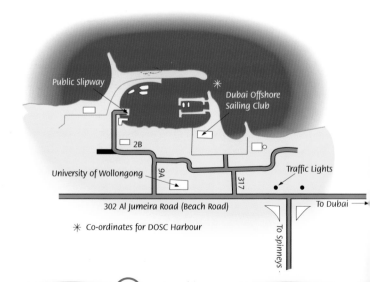

Harbour Maps & Co-ordinates

Sharjah Creek Mouth
Sharjah

N 25° 22' 40"
E 55° 23' 20"

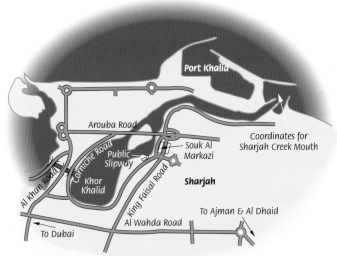

Hamriya Harbour (Umm Al Quwain Slipway)
Umm Al Quwain

N 25° 28' 51"
E 55° 29' 28"

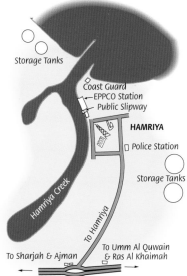

Harbour Maps & Co-ordinates

East Coast

Dibba Bayah Harbour
Dibba (For Musandam)

N 25° 39' 04"
E 56° 16' 12"

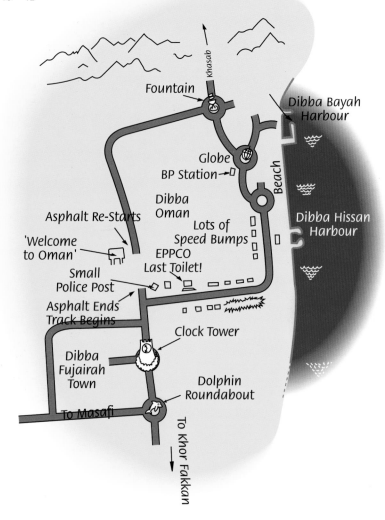

Harbour Maps & Co-ordinates

Khor Fakkan Harbour Slipway
Khor Fakkan

N 25° 20' 53"
E 56° 21' 44"

To Dibba

Ras Lulaya

Oceanic Hotel

Shark Island

Khor Fakkan Port

Khor Fakkan

Public Slipway

To Fujairah

Martini Rock

Ras Qidfa

Qidfa

Lulaya Harbour
Khor Fakkan

N 25° 23' 37"
E 56° 22' 03"

Lulaya

Petrol Station

Oceanic Hotel

Khor Fakkan

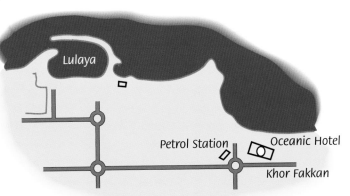

Index

Index

Advertiser Details

Company	Telephone Number	Email/web address
Al Boom Diving	+971-4-342 2993	sbdiving@emirates.net.ae
Al Sawadi Resort	+968-895 545	forumsawadi@interconti.com
Diving House	+971-9-238 3638	dive4fun@emirates.net.ae
Emirates Diving Association	+971-4-393 9390	edadiver@emirates.net.ae
Explorer Publishing	+971-4-391 8060	info@the-explorer.com
FAST (First Aid & Safety Training)	+971-4-282 6470	fastscvs@emirates.net.ae
Federal Express	+971-4-331 4216	www.fedex.com
Grand Stores	+971-4-282 3700	gsdubai@emirates.net.ae
Gulf Marine Sports	+971-2-671 0017	fkabra@hotmail.com
Khasab Travel & Tours	+968-830 464	khastour@omantel.net.om
Masaoods	+971-2-676 0999	mpsdiv@emirates.net.ae
Ocean World Production	+971-4-336 6901	blujex@hotmail.com
Oman Dive Centre	+968-950 261	diveoman@omantel.net.om
Pavilion Dive Centre	+971-4-406 8827	philo@jumeirah-beach.com
Pearl Marine Sports Centre	+971-6-566 3626	pearldiv@emirates.net.ae
Sandy Beach Dive Centre	+971-9-244 5050	sbdiving@emirates.net.ae
Scuba 2000	+971-9-238 8477	dim@emirates.net.ae
Scuba Dubai	+971-4-331 7433	info@scubadubai.com
Scuba International	+971-4-393 7557	scubaint@emirates.net.ae

Explorer Product Range

A to Z Explorer (Dubai)

This is the map book all of Dubai has been waiting for, with concise street names and numbers cross-referenced with a comprehensive A-Z index of businesses, places of interest and tourist attractions. The **Dubai A-Z** is a unique publication that is set to become the standard tool for navigating this ever growing city.

ISBN 976-8182-10-5 • A5 size • 325 pages

Dubai Explorer

The **Dubai Explorer** is the definitive annual lifestyle guide to all that's happening in Dubai. From maps to restaurant reviews, shopping tips to new resident information, it's all presented in the easy to use Explorer Series style. Ideal for anyone visiting or settling in this vibrant and ever changing city, the **Dubai Explorer** lists everything there is to do in Dubai, and more importantly, where to do it.

ISBN 976-8182-33-4 • A5 size • 492 pages

Hand-Held Explorer (Dubai)

The Dubai **Hand-Held Explorer** is the first of Explorer Publishing's travel guides that can be downloaded onto your PDA. Now all the information available in the **Dubai Explorer** can be accessed with the push of a button. Interactive, informative and innovative... the **Hand-Held Explorer** is easy to install, a breeze to use and packed with useful information.

ISBN 976-8182-40-7

Off-Road Explorer (UAE)

An invaluable tool for exploring the UAE's 'outback' with clear and easy to follow instructions. Satellite imagery of every stage of the route is superimposed with the correct track to follow, points of interest, and distances. Stunning photography and advice on driving the more difficult parts complement additional information on topics such as wildlife, safety tips and archaeology.

ISBN 976-8182-37-7 • 210mm x 210mm size • 328 pages

Abu Dhabi Explorer

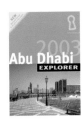

In its third edition, the **Abu Dhabi Explorer** has quickly become the authoritative annual lifestyle guide to all that's going on in Abu Dhabi and the oasis town of Al Ain. It covers everything you need to know about Abu Dhabi and much much more. There really is no alternative to the **Abu Dhabi Explorer** to satisfy your entertainment and leisure needs.

ISBN 976-8182-38-5 • A5 size • 312 pages

Family Explorer (Dubai & Abu Dhabi)

The only family handbook for Dubai and Abu Dhabi – catering specifically to families with children between the ages of 0-14 years. The easy to use Explorer format details the practicalities of family life in the northern Emirates, including information on medical care, education and residence visas. The book also has hundreds of invaluable ideas for indoor and outdoor activities for families and kids.

ISBN 976-8182-34-2 • A5 size • 325 pages

Images of Dubai

Images of Dubai is a visual showcase, sharing the secrets of this remarkable land and introducing newcomers to the wonders of Dubai and the UAE. View architectural details that make the UAE one of the most visually thrilling urban environments in the world, then journey with our photographers along golden beaches under a pastel sunset and deep into the mesmerising sands of the desert.

ISBN 976-8182-37-7 • 290mm x 290mm size • 328 pages

Zappy Explorer (Dubai)

A step-by-step-guide to getting things done in Dubai. The **Zappy Explorer** contains over 100 procedures, tips and advice on all aspects of life, whether business or personal. An indispensable guide explaining in detail how to set up your home or business, apply for various services, and work your way through Dubai's administrative mysteries. The **Zappy Explorer** gives a clear and concise listing of documents required, costs, timings, tips and advice.

ISBN 976-8182-25-3 • 110mm x 250mm size • 375 pages

Emergency Contact Numbers

Service	Dibba (09)	Dubai (04)	Fujairah (09)	Khor Fakkan (09)	Sharjah (06)
Police	244 4211	999	999	999	999
Fire	244 4211	997	997	997	997
Ambulance	244 4210	999	999	999	999
Coastguard	_	345 0260	238 0380	238 6611	528 1667

Diving Doctor

Dr. Horst Kafer - (04 344 2773) Mobile 652 3809
Dr. Jamal Ali Jammal - Dubai Physiotherapy Clinic (04 349 6333)

Hospital	Location	Telephone	Emergency

Ajman

Ajman Hospital	Leewara St	06 743 9333	-

Dubai

Al Maktoum Hospital	Deira	04 222 1211	-
Al Wasl Hospital	Oud Al Metha	04 324 1111	04 306 2444
Rashid Hospital	Bur Dubai	04 337 4000	04 337 4000
American Hospital PRIVATE	Nr Al Nasr Leisureland	04 336 7777	04 309 6645
Welcare Hospital PRIVATE	Nr Princeton Hotel	04 282 7788	04 282 9900

East Coast

Fujairah Medical Centre	Nr Fujairah Hilton	09 223 2555	-
Khor Fakkan Hospital	Nr Lantern R/A	09 237 0222	09 237 0222

Ras Al Khaimah

Saqr Hospital	Al Nakheel Area	07 222 3666	-
Saif Bin Gobash Hospital	Wassit Rd	07 222 3555	07 202 4279

Umm Al Quwain

New Al Qassimi Hospital	Malek Faisal St	06 538 6444	-
Umm Al Quwain Hospital	Nr Al Mussallah R/A	06 765 6888	-

Sharjah

Zahra Hospital Clinic PRIVATE	Al Zahra Square	06 561 9999	-

In an emergency, the hospital staff will decide which hospital you should go to, depending on treatment and the area you live in. There is an air ambulance to major hospitals and a helicopter service is available for mountain and sea rescue.

Safety Points

- Ensure your equipment is regularly serviced
- Clean your equipment thoroughly after each and every dive
- Correctly store your equipment
- DO NOT FLY for 24 hours after diving

A Stunning Photographic Collection...

Images of Dubai is a visual showcase, sharing the secrets of this remarkable land and introducing newcomers to the wonders of Dubai and the United Arab Emirates. Journey with our team of photographers along golden beaches under a pastel sunset, or deep into the mesmerising sands of the desert. View architectural details that make the UAE one of the most visually thrilling urban environments in the world, and dive undersea to encounter the reef creatures who live there. Join us in marvelling at the diversity of astounding locations throughout the seven emirates.

With a refreshingly artistic view of the region, striking images are accompanied by inspired text, further capturing the magic of the varied subject matter. This book is for all those who love this country as well as those who think they might like to...

Available from leading bookstores, hotels, supermarkets or directly from Explorer Publishing. Customised copies and bulk orders ensure generous discounts

Explorer Publishing & Distribution • Dubai Media City • Building 2 • Office 502 • PO Box 34275 • Dubai • UAE
Phone (+971 4) 391 8060 **Fax** (+971 4) 391 8062 **Email** info@explorer-publishing.com **Web** www.explorer-publishing.com

EXPLORER